TWAYNE'S WORLD AUTHORS SERIES

A Survey of the World's Literature

Sylvia E. Bowman, Indiana University
GENERAL EDITOR

FRANCE

Maxwell A. Smith, Guerry Professor of French, Emeritus
The University of Chattanooga
Visiting Professor in Modern Languages
The Florida State University
EDITOR

Paul Claudel

(TWAS 92)

TWAYNE'S WORLD AUTHORS SERIES (TWAS)

The purpose of TWAS is to survey the major writers —novelists, dramatists, historians, poets, philosophers, and critics—of the nations of the world. Among the national literatures covered are those of Australia, Canada, China, Eastern Europe, France, Germany, Greece, India, Italy, Japan, Latin America, New Zealand, Poland, Russia, Scandinavia, Spain, and the African nations, as well as Hebrew, Yiddish, and Latin Classical literatures. This survey is complemented by Twayne's United States Authors Series and English Authors Series.

The intent of each volume in these series is to present a critical-analytical study of the works of the writer; to include biographical and historical material that may be necessary for understanding, appreciation, and critical appraisal of the writer; and to present all material in clear, concise English—but not to vitiate the scholarly content of the work by doing so.

Paul Claudel

By HAROLD A. WATERS

University of Rhode Island

Twayne Publishers, Inc. :: New York

Preface

At the present tally there must be something like fifty four-hundred page volumes of primary Claudel sources. The brevity of this study poses an initial problem but under any conditions introducing the reader to such a huge and variegated opus would be difficult. Should one stress mainly the total amount written, or the general impact of Claudel's literature, or the values of individual works.

Profiting from the autobiographical and thematic qualities of Claudel's work—the first is really an aspect of the second—and also from a referential use of these qualities, I have tried to meet the three goals evenly and adequately. The first two chapters, "Life and times" and "Themes," are designed to explain the meaning of Claudel, and the genre chapters following introduce the single works, one after the other. All are listed, most discussed, which thus gives a quantitative understanding of the overall aim: to introduce the works of Claudel. However space limitations have obliged me to discuss only most briefly Claudel's exegetic prose, that part of his whole opus which the general reader might come to know last anyway.

Rare is the writer who to Claudel's degree so completely recorded his whole being at the moment of writing, and who was so affected by his times and the more immediate contingencies. Paul-André Lesort's excellent *Paul Claudel par lui-même* illustrates this well: The selections forming this collage—"autobiography," besides being mostly in chronological order of composition, tell much of the age in which Claudel lived. In Chapter I only the first forty-odd years are gone into in any detail. With his marriage in 1905 the account evolves to broad lines. Subsequently, the external influences were more normal and predictable, as were consequently his life and of course his work.

Chapter 2 is also a reference table to what follows and it in turn is explainable through Chapter 1. Virtually all Claudel's themes cross genres. The chapter includes style, which in Claudel *is* a theme, down to such prosodic questions as lyricism and the *verset claudélien*. He refashioned the concept, inherited from Baudelaire and Mallarmé, into something divine and all-inclusive. To Claudel it was a universal analogy *under God*. Here is an example of how these space-saving "tables" mesh with each other and with what follows. In "Life and times" one learns of Claudel's Christmas Day conversion. Chapter 2 explains how, in starting from this event, Christmas became a theme in his work. Thereafter, there is no need to go very deeply into the motives behind the Christmas features of specific works, such as the third act of *L'Annonce faite á Marie*, the poem "Le 25 décembre 1886," or the prose work *L'Evangile d'Isaïe*.

As far as I know this is the first total attempt to define Claudel through his themes. Their great importance has been noted by others of course, but they have never been gone into in *number*. Although I am convinced it is *the* way to get at Claudel, treating him thematically has its bad moments. The themes are not all distinct from each other. Two themes may really be identical but seen through different lenses, or one may be an aspect of another. Much of the confusion stems from the Claudelian concept behind them of the divine universal analogy: The cogs of a single machine can look alike.

The concluding chapter tries to situate Claudel from a critical standpoint. My own tastes favor the pros over the cons; I believe in the ultimate fulfillment of Auden's 1939 prophecy, there cited. Some will be interested in learning that Edmund Wilson could not stomach a Claudel play, and that Simone de Beauvoir admitted Claudel has some merit. Interest may change to surprise in the face of Ionesco's lavish praise.

A serious drawback to many of the introductions to Claudel is that they take for granted a certain acquaintance with him on the part of the reader. I have labored not to make a similar assumption. My great hope is that with the help of this study a true beginner can pick up nearly anything by Claudel and recognize what part it is of the total picture. This is the first introduction to Claudel published in the United States.

Casey Point, Rhode Island

HAROLD A. WATERS

Acknowledgments

I am indebted to these publishing houses for their kind permission to quote from the Claudel works indicated: Henry Regnery Company, which holds the American rights on *L'Annonce faite à Marie, Partage de midi, Le Soulier de satin*; Pantheon Books, Inc., which holds the American rights on the Claudel-Gide *Correspondance*; Longmans, Green & Co., which holds the American rights on *Seigneur, apprenez-nous à prier*; Mercure de France, which holds the copyrights on *Vers d'exil, Connaissance de l'Est, Tête d'or, La Ville, La Jeune Fille Violaine, L'Echange*; Editions Gallimard, which holds all the other copyrights on Claudel's published works. I am also indebted to the Société Paul Claudel of Paris, which let me use its archives when I wanted, notably to read parts of the manuscript of the *Journal*. Most of all to two of the Société's officers, Monsieur Pierre Claudel (a son of the poet) and Madame Renée Nantet (a daughter), who both warmly extended to me considerable assistance and counsel. The University of Rhode Island accorded me a Summer Faculty Fellowship and a travel grant, which allowed me to work on this study in Paris during the summer of 1965; subsequently, I received another grant-in-aid from the University for secretarial expenses. My wife Lenore was a fine Girl Friday. Professor William Matheson of Brandeis University generously gave my manuscript a close reading, and I thank him for much sound advice.

Contents

Chronology

(Dates of first publication are provided and indicated as such when composition dates are not known.)

1862- Villeneuve-sur-Fère (Aisne). 1862: marriage of Louis-
1870 Prosper Claudel and Louise Cerveaux. 1864: birth of Camille Claudel. 1866: birth of Louise Claudel. 1868: birth of Paul-Louis-Charles-Marie Claudel, August 6.

1870- Family lives in three other provincial locations. 1880:
1882 Claudel's first communion, marking the end of his religious practices. 1881: on a return to Villeneuve witnesses death of maternal grandfather.

1882- Paris. Mme Claudel and the three children settle there
1893 to let Camille study sculpture. Virtually on arrival Claudel loses faith. 1883: though winner of one scholastic prize at the lycée Louis-le-Grand—awarded in person by Renan—fails first part of baccalauréat, but passes it next year. 1885: passes final part, in philosophy. 1886: reads *Illuminations*; writes *L'Endormie*; reads *Une Saison en enfer*; faith returns on Christmas Day in Notre Dame; same day accidently opens a Bible. 1887: begins sometime attendance at Mallarmé's "mardis." 1888: *Une Mort prématurée*. 1889: *Tête d'or* (1st v.); begins studies at the *Ecole des Sciences Politiques*. 1886-1890: *Premiers Vers*. 1890: first place, examination for entrance to diplomatic service; Christmas Day "second" communion marks formal return to Church; *La Ville* (1st v.). 1892-1893: *La Jeune Fille Violaine* (1st v.).

1893- New York and Boston. Consular posts. 1892-1894: trans-
1895 lates *Agamemnon*. 1893-1894: *L'Echange* (1st v.). 1894: *Tête d'or* (2nd v.).

1895- First China period. 1895: *Vers d'exil*. 1895-1896: *Le Repos*
1899 *du septième jour*. 1897: *La Ville* (2nd v.).

1900 Return to France: 1898-1900: *La Jeune Fille Violaine* (2nd v.). Brief retreats at Solesmes, Ligugé. En route for China aboard *Ernest Simons*, meets "Ysé."

11

1900- Second China period. 1900-1904: *Art poétique*. 1904:
1905   breaks with "Ysé." 1895-1905: *Connaissance de l'Est*.
1905- Return to France. 1905: *Partage de midi* (1st v.). 1906:
1906   demonstrates against the Inventories; weds Reine Sainte-
       Marie-Perrin on March 15, and they leave three days
       later for China.
1906- Third China period. 1907: birth of Marie Claudel. 1900-
1909   1908: *Cinq Grandes Odes*. 1908: birth of Pierre Claudel.
1909- Prague. 1910: birth of Reine Claudel. 1908-1910: *L'Otage*.
1911   1910-1911: *L'Annonce faite à Marie* (1st v.).
1912- Frankfort and Hamburg. 1911-1912: *La Cantate à trois
1914   voix*. 1912: birth of Henri Claudel. 1913: *Protée*; death of
       father; Camille Claudel confined. 1887-1914: *Corona be-
       nignitatis anni Dei*. 1913-1914: *Le Pain dur*.
1915- Paris and Rome. 1913-1915: translates *The choephori*.
1916   1913-1916: translates *The eumenides*. 1915-1916: *Le Père
       humilié*.
1917- Rio de Janeiro. 1917: birth of Renée Claudel.
1918
1919- Copenhagen.
1921
1921- Tokyo. First ambassadorship. 1919-1924: *Le Soulier de
1927   satin*. 1910-1925: *Feuilles de saints*. 1925: *Cent Phrases
       pour éventails*. 1925-1926: visits Europe.
1927- Washington, various returns to France. 1927: buys châ-
1933   teau of Brangues (Isère); *Le Livre de Christophe Colomb*.
       1925-1928: *Conversations dans le Loir-et-Cher*. 1929:
       death of mother. 1928-1932: *Au milieu des vitraux de
       l'Apocalypse*. 1905-1933: *Positions et propositions, I* and
       II.
1933- Brussels. 1934: *Jeanne d'Arc au bûcher*.
1935
1935- Retirement. Residences in Paris and Brangues. 1933-1935:
1955   *Un Poète regarde la Croix*. 1926-1936: *Figures et para-
       boles*. 1931-1936: *Les Aventures de Sophie*. 1935-1937:
       L'Epée et le miroir. 1937: *Du sens figuré de l'Ecriture*.
       1938: *L'Histoire de Tobie et de Sara*. 1908-1939: *Présence
       et prophétie*. 1913-1939: *Contacts et circonstances*. 1940-
       1942: *Paul Claudel interroge l'APOCALYPSE*. 1942: *Seig-
       neur, apprenez-nous à prier*. 1942-1943: *Le Soulier de*

satin (2nd v.). 1915-1944: *Poèmes de guerre.* 1927-1944: *Visages radieux.* 1934-1945: *L'OEil écoute.* 1943-1945: *Le Cantique des cantiques.* 1944-1946: *La Rose et le rosaire.* 1946: *Introduction à l'APOCALYPSE: Le Livre de Job* (publ.). 1946-1947: *Discours et remerciements.* 1927-1948: *Accompagnements.* 1946-1948: *Emmaüs.* 1948: *Partage de midi* (2nd v.); *L'Annonce faite à Marie* (2nd v.). 1949: *Partage de midi* (3rd v.). 1948-1950: *L'Evangile d'Isaïe.* 1950-1951: *L'Echange* (2nd v.). 1951: *Trois Figures saintes pour le temps actuel.* 1951-1952: *Mémoires improvisés.* 1949-1954: *J'aime la Bible.* 1905-1955: *Journal* 1918-1955: *Psaumes.* Death of Claudel, February 23, 1955.

CHAPTER 1

Life and Times[1]

P AUL Claudel was born on August 6, 1868, in Villeneuve-sur-
Fère, an agricultural village in the department of Aisne so
miniscule that no conventional map of all France shows it. His
father, Louis-Prosper, a fiscal functionary from La Bresse in the
Vosges, had been sent in 1860 as tax collector to Villeneuve,
where in 1862 he married Louise Cerveaux, daughter of the
Villeneuve physician and niece of the village priest. Claudel was
the fourth and last child. Henri was born and died in 1863,
Camille was born in 1864, Louise in 1866. Claudel sometimes
referred to his peasant forebears, but his ancestral background
was mostly middle-class. On the other hand, until his fifteenth
year he was exposed only to Villeneuve and other rural spots also
near the old province of Champagne. In a certain sense he was
a peasant by environment, indelibly so. Claudel's voice was often
recorded in his later years. One is amazed to hear the Champe-
nois dominance in the voice of the ethereal poet and three-time
ambassador.

I Villeneuve-sur-Fère

A simple listing of Claudel's residences as a youth would hide
the importance of his birthplace. He left Villeneuve at the age
of two never to "live" there again. The village had not even
been his mother's birthplace. In 1870 Louis-Prosper was sent to
Bar-le-Duc (Meuse), in 1876 to Nogent-sur-Seine (Aube), in
1879 to Wassy-sur-Blaise (Haute-Marne). His family accompanied him to each new post. In 1882 the elder daughter's artistic
leanings took Mme Claudel and the children to Paris, where
Camille could study sculpture formally. Thenceforward, the
whole family was reunited only on occasion.

What bound the poet to Villeneuve was a house. After the marriage of Claudel's parents, Father Cerveaux had domiciled them

15

in the rectory, where Paul and his siblings were born. Meanwhile, the priest had had a house of his own built. His niece and nephew-in-law inherited it on his death in 1869, and moved in. Thus Villeneuve became more Louis-Prosper's home than his birthplace of La Bresse. Before and after the 1882 shift to Paris, Claudel vacationed in, gravitated to, either La Bresse or Ville- neuve, especially the latter. For instance, in 1881 he returned to his birthplace when his maternal grandfather was dying from cancer and actually witnessed the last throes. Between 1893 and 1935 Claudel as a diplomat spent most of his time abroad, but until the former date—when he was twenty-five—Villeneuve was certainly of great importance to him. During his long career, he was progressively less attached to his birthplace. Before his first departure from France, it was the most vital place in the world to him. By his retirement in 1935, experience had put it at the eye-end of the telescope. His first full-length play, the first version of *Tête d'or* (1889; *Golden head*), begins in a setting greatly like the environs of Villeneuve, but an incomplete third version of 1951 begins in a World War II German stalag.[2]

Villeneuve is some sixty miles northwest of Paris as the crow flies. Its own small region, the Tardenois, is sandwiched between l'Ile-de-France and la Champagne. A very striking feature of the village—now, and it must also have been at the end of the nine- teenth century—is its isolation. The nearest railway station is some four miles away at Fère-en-Tardenois, and in our present times if one walks the distance one may see only one or two cars in mo- tion on the road. There is no bus service. Houses rim the large central square. A few houses border the lanes and narrow roads at the outskirts. One of these ways leads toward the nearby medieval farm of Combernon, another toward Le Géyn—Le Géant, or The Giant—both familiar places in the Violaine plays. When there are no more houses, the vistas consist of descending fields and woodlands: Villeneuve is on a modest hill. A typical house in the village proper is a sort of duplex. Next to the resi- dence is a stable and hayloft. Herds of cows are guided by their owners through the rough streets, the men perhaps acknowledg- ing a stranger, but the women studiously avoiding a stranger's eyes. In "Mon Pays" (1938; "Where I grew up"; in *Contacts et circonstances*), Claudel effectively describes his native village. The forests were dark, the peasants hardworking. Acutely exposed to the elements through its hilltop position, Villeneuve provided the poet-to-be with a combined material and spiritual outlook upon all existence. Claudel's Villeneuve-sur-Fère brings to mind the ambience of *Wuthering Heights*.

II *Early Relocations*

Claudel's family life did not alleviate the grim aspects of Villeneuve, nor did the frequent childhood relocations. No two in the family got on well. His parents were not talkative. Any combination of the five Claudels brought on friction and quarrelling. His Violaine plot, the two versions of *La Jeune Fille Violaine* (1892-1893, 1898-1900; *The maiden Violaine*) and *L'Annonce faite à Marie* (1910-1911; *The tidings brought to Mary*), depicts a traditional sister rivalry, but Violaine the good sister owes little to either Camille or Louise, whereas to an extent the bad sister Mara (or Bibiane) is indebted to them both. As late as 1904, Louis-Prosper wrote to his son: "How unfortunate that these discussions, the family discords cause me such deep chagrin. If you could help me reestablish harmony, what a favor you would do me!"[3] Claudel was impatient and querulous like the rest. His early taste for solitude did serve to spare him some emotional wear and tear. The impatience became a lifetime fixture. Years later, Claudel the consul would peremptorily eject people from his office. He reacted to literary critics with gusto. His solitariness too remained with him, making of him not always the warmest of friends. There is little *tutoiement* in his published correspondence. Later, when he became mellower and more "lovable," it was still despite a ready temper. In personality, Claudel was a Gallic Harry Truman. The elder sister Camille was headstrong; Louise the second-oldest specialized in making her own opinions prevail; Louis-Prosper was haughty and silent; Mme Claudel was severe and silent.

Paul Claudel's education before Paris was ordinary. Some public schooling; some training under nuns; and for a while he shared a tutor with his sisters. Louise was almost a freethinker and the rest were not particularly religious. For many Frenchmen the first communion is more social than sacramental, and as Claudel remarked in "Ma Conversion" (1909), it represented "both the highpoint and the end of my religious practices" (*Con-*

tacts; XVI, 189). He read voraciously in his solitude and also
hiked a good deal. In 1881 he was already acquainted with
Shakespeare, whose blank verse may well have exerted an effect
on his prosody. Before or shortly after his 1882 arrival in Paris,
he became well grounded in many other great names of literature
and philosophy—among them Aristotle, Racine, and Dante. Symbolist and Naturalist currents were in their heyday during his
youth, and he kept up with them, starting at an early age. The
two movements were not totally antipathetic to each other. If
the life of the mind was for the Symbolists the truest life, the
Naturalists were helping lay the groundwork for the science of
psychology. Naturalism did not really eschew art. Perhaps the
greatest convergence was their mutual tendency toward a non-
divine idealism. In general the Symbolists aspired to a perfection
of this world, yet not of it, in the sense that it was sought by
human means but was unattainable. The Naturalists entertained
hopes of social amelioration by human effort, hopes which could
be realized only imperfectly because what they understood as
determinism was relatively unscientific. Either they did not seize
all the causal factors of a given situation, or they had the wrong
ones in the first place.

III *Materialism, Paris, Loss of Faith*

So Claudel read Hugo, Goethe, Renan, Voltaire, Balzac, Keats,
Baudelaire, everything apparently he could lay his hands on,
including the French translation of Alban Butler's *Lives of the
saints*. Readings except the latter were largely responsible for his
cessation of religious practices. They are not necessarily "culprits"
in this. It is more a question of a chemical formula. What Claudel
did or absorbed in his youth combined with Claudel the individual to produce the religion-less youth of fourteen who came to
Paris in 1882 and, concurrent with his entrance into Louis-le-
Grand, stopped believing as well. He wrote in "Ma Conversion":

Reading Renan's *Life of Jesus* furnished new pretexts to that change
in convictions which, furthermore, everything about me facilitated or
encouraged. Let one remember those sad '80's, the age when Naturalism had its widest success. Never did matter's yoke seem surer. Everything meriting a name—in art, science, and literature—was irreligious.
All the (self-styled) great men of that waning century had distin-

guished themselves by their hostility toward the Church. Renan was king (XVI, 189-190).

Over the next four years he aped the spirit of his times. Life at home stayed the same. The adolescent *lycéen* was "extremely unhappy ... because of the absence of education. The absence of an aliment whose need I sensed made me suffer intensely."[4] Once he even put a pistol to his head. At Louis-le-Grand he skipped a year but paid for this by failing his examination for the first baccalauréat in 1883; though failing he won one prize, handed him by Renan in person at the graduation ceremonies.

The year 1886 was the most important in his life. When he began to write is not clear. His earliest surviving literary efforts date from then, the one-act *Endormie* (*The sleeping one*)[5] and one poem of his *Premiers Vers*, "Pour la messe des hommes dernier sacrifice d'amour!" ("For the mass of men, love's last sacrifice!") The play shows Claudel already en route to his variably-lengthed lyric line, the *vers* or the *verset claudélien*:

> Sometime he leaps aside grimacing,
> Like a tomcat in love,
> Sometimes he shakes his hands
> As if he'd just touched a toad.

> Quelquefois il saute de côté en grimaçant,
> Comme un matou amoureux.
> Quelquefois il secoue ses mains
> Comme s'il venait de toucher un crapaud (VI, 41).

These early similes are perhaps attempts to imitate Baudelaire, whom he had started reading two years before at the age of sixteen. As for the poem, it is written in strict *alternance*, with quatrains of *alexandrins embrassés*. Indeed, the *Premiers Vers* (1886-1900) and the *Vers d'exil* (1895) are all extremely traditional in form.

IV *Rimbaud and Notre Dame*

It was not these modest steps that made 1886 so important to him. First, it was the discovery of Rimbaud through two issues of the periodical *La Vogue: Illuminations*, then *Une Saison en enfer*. Many discredit Isabelle Rimbaud's claim of her brother's deathbed conversion. Some are disinclined to read belief in his

iconoclastic writings. Be that as it may, consciously or unconsciously Claudel saw in Rimbaud a suffering individual deeply
touched with divine grace. His encounter with the two works
prepared him for an event he has described many times, detail
by detail in "Ma Conversion," poetically in "Le 25 décembre
1886" (1942; *Visages radieux*). The dilettante Claudel went twice
to Notre Dame on Christmas Day, 1886, in order to reap the cere-
monial value of the observances. The prose account relates how,
as the Magnificat was being sung during Vespers, there occurred

the event which dominates my whole life. In a single instant my heart
was touched and *I believed*. I believed . . . with a certitude that left
no room for doubt, so that, since then, all the reasonings, all the
chances of an agitated life, haven't been able to shake my faith, nor,
truthfully, to touch it (XVI, 191).

Still another event was reserved for him that day; here is how
he described it fifty years later in *J'aime la Bible* (1949-1954):

And later, in the evening of that unforgettable Christmas Day of
1886, how can one fail to see divine intervention in that Bible, a gift
to my sister Camille from one of her Protestant friends, which was
there on the table? I opened it, something I had never done before,
and at two places. The first was the story of Emmaus in Saint Luke,
when the Lord, as night came on, opened to his two trembling com-
panions the secrets of the Old Testament. The second was that
sublime chapter VIII of Proverbs which is used as the Epistle on
Immaculate Conception. Ah! It didn't take me long to recognize in
that radiant face the triple and inseparable evocation of the features
of the Mother of God, of the Church, and of God's Wisdom. Not a
single woman in my subsequent dramas has failed to show the traces
of that dazzling insight (XXI, 350).

From then on, a Bible was his constant companion: And it is
indeed difficult to find a woman in his plays who does not to a
degree incarnate the three mentioned entities.

From the outset Claudel sensed that he and Rimbaud were
kindred spirits. They surely were. Both grew up in the provinces,
and Rimbaud's Ardennes borders on Claudel's Aisne. Their
mothers were somber, silent, humorless. Home life was generally
unpleasant. Neither liked the times. If at first Rimbaud was a
communard, later on he wrote that "la vraie vie est absente":
"true life is elsewhere." Both were precocious, solitary, great read-

ers, cross-country walkers. They both reached Paris at about the same age. And of course both were poetic geniuses. It is probably better to leave well enough alone, to accept that Claudel saw in Rimbaud a believer full of grace. At any rate, the contact was magical, and was greatly responsible for Claudel's frame of mind that led to his instantaneous conversion on Christmas Day, 1886. It should be stressed, though, that since in that year he did not know the whole anecdotal and literary Rimbaud, the basic debt hinged on his reading in 1886 of *Illuminations* and *Une Saison en enfer.*

Looking back at this part of his life, Claudel consistently felt that until the end of 1886 his inherent calling to be one of God's creatures had been violated by his own nature and by the elements round him, notably: those he associated with, his education, the spirit of the times. That is, he had been both outer- and inner-directed. Thenceforth, his life was to be mainly inner-motivated, in terms of his interpretation of divine will. He felt great guilt for his four years of disbelief and for his pre-1882 self. He was also to resent immensely those external factors he held responsible for what he had been before his reconversion.

Claudel's abrupt change-of-heart is similar to René's in Chateaubriand's novel. René's *mal du siècle* was also corrected by a sudden revelation. But if René's gropings ended then and there, Claudel had first to recognize then purge that within him which was not really himself. In addition, he had to tame or overcome aspects of his own nature. It took four years to the day. His Christmas 1890 communion at Notre Dame marked his formal return to the fold. It would have been earlier, had it not been for his pride. A confessor had insisted that he reveal his intention to his family and this he had put off for a considerable time. In 1886 Claudel re-believed in God. In 1890 he fully believed what he had tried to believe fully for four years: that he had to be a member of the Roman Catholic Church, had to accept all its teachings, had to act as he was commanded by either the Church or by divine will.

Literally, Claudel came out of this period an apocalyptic Christian. He was too horrified by his times, too impressed by how his fate had changed, too close to his God not to look on life on earth in a dramatic, apocalyptic way. He often thought of the road to Tarsus; this was more than a convenient analogy based on the similar experience of a namesake. Just as he had been a voracious reader, Claudel absorbed his religion with such applied thoroughness that, without a hint of bad taste, his works abound in references to the digestibility of all matters of faith. For example, in the poem "Sainte Claire" (publ. 1947; *Visages radieux*) divine light is described as "edible." From the beginning to the end of his life Claudel ate and drank heartily. This no doubt played a role in his alimentary metaphors. He once wrote to Jacques Rivière: "Why think one's conscience and one's stomach are made in different ways?"[6]

V Artistic First Steps

The four years from 1886 to 1890 brought him to the brink of artistic greatness. His three dramatic attempts of the period are *Fragment d'un drame* (1888), also referred to as *Une Mort prématurée* (*A premature death*), and the first versions of *Tête d'or* (1889) and *La Ville* (1889; *The city*). These inchoate works are extremely autobiographical, particularly the first-mentioned. This explains perhaps why he destroyed the rest of it. The plot depicts an incestuous parricide en route to his death, reflecting no doubt suicidal thoughts on the part of the author. As for the incest, all of us have all sorts of thoughts. The distinction here is between normal thoughts and atypical actions.

When Simon Agnel, the hero of the second play, ultimately becomes an Alexander-like figure, his long blond tresses earn him the nickname of Tête d'or, or Golden Head. This character leaves a place like Villeneuve full of materialistic thoughts that are corrected only at the end, when he is dying, by a Princess, who quite evidently embodies all the qualities Claudel said he put into his dramatic women.

In *La Ville* the poet Coeuvre (Coeuvres is a place-name near Villeneuve) advises the workers of the materialistic City to cast off their shackles. When they do so, they sink into anarchy. Then religious forces rise to anoint a ruling prince. This play expands on the simpler *Tête d'or*, which reflects Claudel's "taming" by God; now the message is of the need for a Christian state. Thus the progression is from plain belief, quietistic perhaps, to the position that belief must be lived. The autobiographical connotations are clear.

Tête d'or and *La Ville* are ill-formed, but these first two complete dramas show Claudel to be already in command of his lyric line, whose technics will be dwelt on more lengthily in the next chapter. Summarily, it is free verse, each *verset* containing one or more groups of words or syllables, the stress or stresses falling usually where they fall usually in French. The length and contents obey free verse principles and also—very especially—dictates arising from the poet's particular state of receptivity. The line thus contains elements that are conscious, others that are unconscious; it is both psychological and physiological. The oxymoron "psychological breath" is a good short description of it.

In 1887 Claudel began infrequent attendance at Mallarmé's "mardis." There he met many others eventually to become famous, notably Valéry and Gide. Traditional poetry was on trial. Those who came were not really jury members: They came as spectators, listening to their host-judge destroy and create. These sessions helped put a capstone on Claudel's lesson from Symbolism. Constantly in his writings one comes on the seminal question apparently often asked by the Master: *"Qu'est-ce que CELA veut dire?" "*What does *that* mean?"*[7] Already Baudelaire's image associations and Rimbaud's application of his own theoretical "disordered unleashing of the senses" had made of Claudel a budding *voyant* or seer in a very primitivistic way. The "thing" 's message was both in itself and in the mind and eyes of the beholder, who must work intensely and closely with these elements if he is to express the thing in terms of the known, that is, with basic analogics. Baudelaire used many concepts in his poetry— God, the Devil, perfection, damnation. Another concept was the universal analogy. He was fundamentally, then, an artist using concepts. What Claudel's conversion experience meant to him as a poet was that for himself Baudelaire's superficial involvement with concepts was insufficient. Later—one does not know exactly when—Claudel fastened onto the phrase from Ecclesiasticus, *"Nec impedias musicam"*—"Do not hinder the music" (sometimes *non* or *ne* instead of *nec*). It was to become a life motto. At the end of 1886, Claudel was on the way to seeing the universal analogy in a more specialized way still, but at precisely that time it was for him the idea of an orchestrated unity planned by God and under God, a *divine* universal analogy. Mallarmé taught that receptivity and reliance upon the senses were the ways toward

the prime question's answer. His principal textbook could be
said to be *Les Fleurs du mal.* It was surely that of Claudel, upon
whom Baudelaire's "Correspondances" seems to have exerted a
direct and dynamic influence. With the help of Rimbaud, and
because of his conversion-in-the-bud, Claudel while listening to
the Master was rephrasing the question into: "What does *God*
mean by *that?*"

In 1889 Claudel switched from law to political science. He now
intended to become a Foreign Service interpreter specializing in
Eastern tongues. However, the first examinations he could take
qualified for consulate duties. These he took, in 1890, and won
highest mention. During his training he met and was befriended
by the great French statesman Philippe Berthelot. The friendship
later proved invaluable. A budding militant Catholic, Claudel
was to develop in a consular service that was part of a government just as bellicosely devoted to absolute separation of church
and state. Part of what Claudel published in the early period
appeared without his name, sometimes for this reason, sometimes
because there were regulations against public publication by one
in his position. Of course, those who ruled his professional destiny were well aware of his writing activities, and of other of his
nonprofessional activities. For instance, on leave in France in
1906, he took part in three public demonstrations against inven-
tory committees. As his reputation waxed, Claudel was more able
to stand on his own two feet, but until 1910 or thereabouts
Berthelot's behind-the-scenes support proved invaluable to en-
able Claudel to stay in the Foreign Service in the first place and
secondly to allow him to garner the more-than-satisfactory pro-
motions and interesting assignments in spite of all.

During his training period he continued to read widely in a
manner fairly undirected save for two areas of concentration, the
Greek classics and religious works, notably those with a mystic
orientation—for example, *The imitation of Jesus Christ* and the
Pensées. His interest in mysticism is reflected in the play he wrote
at this time, the first version of *La Jeune Fille Violaine* (1892-
1893). Here again the Villeneuve region figures importantly. The
action centers on Le Géyn and Combernon, and Violaine is actually a nearby place-name. *Violaine* is certainly a product of its
author's life. For one thing, it presents or teaches a basic Catholicism, in that its main family—the Vercors—is so well-knit and so

religiously oriented. His interest in mysticism is seen in the saint and thaumaturge that the heroine becomes. One of the many influences of the art of the times is its Symbolist atemporality, shared, incidentally, by the first *Tête d'or*. The plot is easier to follow than those of his two preceding full-blown efforts: In many ways already as great a poet as he was ever to be, Claudel was also maturing as a master dramatist. He probably read Whitman for the first time in 1886, for that poet appeared in translation in one of the two "Rimbaud" issues of *La Vogue*. Perhaps Whitman, along with the Bible and Shakesperean blank verse, reinforced Claudel's faith in his own poetic line.

In his correspondence and in his *Journal* Claudel was wont to grumble about the insufficient recognition of his artistic genius. The facts do not bear out his complaint, which must be relegated to human nature. In this modest training period (for both careers) of 1890 through 1893 and before he had reached the age of twenty-five, Claudel received "rave" letters from many of the then literary greats, some of whom were such objects of his respect that their influence on his work is undebatable. Apropos of *Tête d'or*, in 1890 Maeterlinck—if the play's mythical quality is Wagnerian, its atemporality is certainly due to him—told many of his friends and acquaintances he was simply overwhelmed. To Claudel himself he wrote: "I am beginning to believe it is genius in the most undeniable form it has ever worn."[8] And in 1893 Mallarmé wrote, in a virtual pastiche of his own style: "The place [which is the] Theater [which place is] insufficient to [represent] the tragedy of Life, the mystery of which [that is, Life's] music and words alone express, you are one of those who will have superbly transposed that place in the book, notably by *La Ville*." While in general published criticism on Claudel was scarce in the early years, in 1892—when Claudel was only twenty-three—three highly laudatory articles in Dutch by M.-G. Byvanck appeared in the *Nederlansche Spectator* (nos. 27, 30, 34).

VI Diplomatic Beginnings

His first consular post, underpaid, was in New York, in 1893. The next year he moved on to Boston. He left the country in 1895. As an ardent Catholic, a budding monarchist, an enemy of realism and materialism, a friend of tradition, he was bound to

dislike America. So he did, according to his own account in
Mémoires improvisés,[9] and the second *Jeune Fille Violaine* (1898-
1900; see act IV). On the other hand, contemporary letters to his
friend Maurice Pottecher show a touristic and youthful fascination with the United States.[10] The situation was bad: wretched
pay, confinement within the same four walls for the first time in
his life over long stretches of time. But insofar as America itself
was responsible for his first opinions about it, it is more exact to
say that there were many sorts of likes and dislikes in his feelings,
most of them fairly predictable. Claudel's subsequent ideas and
feelings colored the initial real ones. Suffice it to say that Claudel
was far from the time in his life when he would be able to accept
all of creation in a more benign frame of mind. His personal reaction against America was based on the more pleasant simplicity
and tranquillity of the Europe he had left behind, and on America's relative non-Catholicism and its materialism. Much later, although he never as a true Symbolist lost completely his yearnings
for the ideal, he came to believe that there is a purpose in "progress," and to accept the country of his first consular post as a
manifestation of divine will.

Much else also occupied his mind when he was in the United
States. His attraction to the Latin and Greek classics had now
centered on Aeschylus. In France he had started and in America
terminated a translation of *Agamemnon* (1892-1894), based both
on his knowledge of Greek and on a literal prose translation. He
also wrote the first version of *L'Echange* (1893-1894), his "American" drama but paradoxical in that—under the influence of
Aeschylus—it is also his most "classical" play, with a cast limited
to four and a plot true to the unities. In the play, scandalous
America comes off poorly, but commercial America is shown in
an advantageous light. Commercialism is an important key to
understanding Claudel's personal evolution. His reaction against
what he deemed scabrous shows what in him was already fixed
forever. But in the approval of commerce, a Claudel is revealed
who was learning to like business and who was beginning to
become a businessman himself. One could say he was becoming
true to his own bourgeois origins; henceforth he was always to
be a champion of the status quo. In 1894 he wrote a second version of *Tête d'or*, a sort of clarification of the first. Apropos of it
he wrote to Pottecher: "I intend to compose in the same way

series of editions of my dramas. In art nothing is definitive. I once thought the opposite was true."[11] Until the end Claudel wrote and rewrote his plays. *La Jeune Fille Violaine* was to see five forms, each of which was considered by him as an integral work of art. Subsequent versions mark two sorts of departures. There are those through the 1910-1911 *Annonce faite à Marie* (*The tidings Brought to Mary*)—the third Violaine play—where one feels that Claudel still related to the previous efforts. Artistically, these new versions show changes that attempt to better rather the dramatic than the poetic qualities. As for thought, one sees certain ideas muted, others more heavily stressed, some new ones introduced. The new versions of his old age show a different trend. For example, the 1951 *Echange* reveals an author far removed in mind as well as in time from a situation of almost sixty years previous; this eviscerated play is an attempted parable. All his latter-day versions are too far removed from the initial ones to be much concerned with them beyond their basic plots.

In 1895 he returned to France, then left for China and did not see his homeland again until 1899. The nostalgia of his American sojourn recurred in his *Vers d'exil* (1895), and he also began composing the prose-poems of *Connaissance de l'Est* (1895-1905; *The East I know*). These last mark a formal attempt to explain aspects of China through a lens carved in part by Symbolism, partly by Saint Thomas Aquinas: For he had brought with him the two *Summas* and over this period read them thoroughly. *Connaissance* is in effect a midway station on the way toward an objective presentation of his own art which soon saw fruition in *Art poétique* (1900-1904). While in China he began exchanging letters with André Gide, and with Francis Jammes. These epistles are naturally not the first important ones in his life, but they are the earliest protracted series to have seen print and Claudel's correspondence is a subgenre of his prose that is gaining ever-increasing attention. For over two decades Claudel tried and failed to convert Gide. The proselytizer in Claudel was pronounced from the moment he had something to dispense; this was in the 1890's and the product was of course Catholicism. There were extraliterary aspects to this activity of a man whose works so utterly reflect himself at the instant of composition; his desire to bring his reader or spectator to his God and Church was a permanent companion of his pen.

Three events in his life dominated a few short years at the beginning of the twentieth century. Their influence is discernible in his work from the moment of their occurrence until his death, either as a major theme or as a strong contrapuntal element. By 1906 Claudel's outlook was formed and other incidents of those years are so dwarfed as to merit only passing mention, if any at all. Consequently the rest of the chapter deals almost exclusively with these three matters, plus the crucial turning point of the late 1920's. These three matters are Claudel's rejected vocation, his great sin, and his marriage.

VII   The Would-be Priest

While Claudel's readings on religious subjects had served mainly to better acquaint him with the God and Church which had come to be his, they had also fanned a spark that had ignited probably very soon after his conversion. The hustle and industrial ugliness of the United States had strengthened Claudel's fleeting desire to quit his century. Now China, in whose tranquillity Claudel delighted, gave him ample opportunity to contemplate the next step. There is an understandable connection between the desire to proselytize, growing within him at this time, and the desire to be a priest. In China also, he met several missionaries he admired; these men no doubt helped sway his inclinations simply by their example. Expectedly, his three plays of the period reflect such preoccupations. At the end of *Le Repos du septième jour* (1896; *And on the seventh day God rested*) the old Emperor abdicates in favor of his son and heads penniless for "the Mountain." The second version of *La Ville* (1897) has a significant change in that now the poet Coeuvre becomes the City's bishop. A telling addition in the second *Jeune Fille Violaine* (1898-1900) is the priest-like church-builder Pierre de Craon, a celibate who is in many other ways also separated from his century. He is largely responsible for inspiring the heroine to assume a saintly role. Indeed, separation had already been a theme of the 1892-1893 Violaine play, through the title character's life apart as a hermit and through her father's abandonment of his earthly possessions. Some of the prose-poems of the contemporary *Connaissance de l'Est*, notably "Pensée en mer" ("Thought on the high seas") and "Le Sédentaire," also have separation as theme.

Claudel returned to France in January 1900. In September he entered the Benedictine monastery at Solesmes (Sarthe). A passage in *Cinq Grandes Odes,* which he began there, shows him on the point of giving up art forever, provided only that his calling be authentic. For an unknown reason, in the same month he moved to another Benedictine abbey, at Ligugé (Vienne); there he met J.-K. Huysmans, who was writing a book on Saint Colette of Corbie.[12] But he left after only a week, with the sorry realization that he was not meant to be a priest. Nevertheless, sacerdotal qualities crop up frequently in his writings. His theater characters of either sex often seem to be orating from a pulpit. When late in life he filled out the so-called Marcel Proust questionnaire, after "Who would you have liked to be?" he wrote "A priest."

VIII   *The Great Sin*

If the events of September 1900 find many echoes in his works, those beginning in October of the same year far outshadow them. In that month Claudel left again for China. Aboardship, perhaps it was during a game of hunt-the-slipper, he came to know a young married woman who with her husband and children was also bound for China. It was a fateful encounter. In China she left her family for Claudel. Their union lasted four years, until October 1904. It is harrowingly described in *Partage de midi* (1905), a play often too close to life to be lyrical in any conventional way but which is a moving tone-poem intended by Claudel to depict physical love as being fraught with harsh dangers. The title is most complex. "Partage" means share or sharing, division or equal division, split or break. "Midi" means noon, and in this instance many figurative extensions thereof. One may think of the first part of Valéry's *Cimetière marin,* or of the opening words of the *Divine comedy.* The hero is Mesa, associable with the Latin *mensa*—a table or something flat. Mesa's vocation has just been rejected and his spirit has been leveled (to level: *faire table rase*). The decisive meeting occurs at high noon on a still sea with the skies and waters divided equally by the ship. Mesa is silent, solitary, halfway through life, and a new career awaits him. The title is thus in certain ways tautological. Ysé is the heroine. An important aspect of her name is its cutting sound.

Another is the sword-likeness of the letter Y. On two levels, at least, Ysé pierces Mesa. Until this experience woman had been for Claudel a symbol or agent of inspiration and divine love. Now she also represented human love. In terms of Pascal's "Il n'y a pas deux amours!" ("There are not two sorts of love!"), Mesa's and Ysé's union implies either a contradiction or a paradox. Claudel decided it was the latter, that humans create between themselves an earthly love that can ultimately be channeled toward God. From this time the Beatrice motif became a physical part of him and of his work.[13] The ethereal Princess of the two *Tête d'or*, Lâla of the second *Ville*, the two Violaines, would now be joined by heartier Claudelian heroines. Decades later, *Le Soulier de satin* (1919-1924; *The satin slipper*) was to have appended before the text: "*Deus escreve direito por linhas tortas, proverbe portugais; Etiam peccata*, Saint Augustin." ("God writes straight with crooked lines"; "Sins also serve.") As Claudel saw it, in a God-created universe sin must play a paradoxical role in the cause of good. One reading of *Cinq Grandes Odes*—whose composition coincides largely with this crucial period—makes of these long poems virtually a five-act play: The narrator is transported from being a pre-Ysé harkener of his divine muse into the experience itself, then partially resolves the paradox, then relapses in favor of the last throes of earthly love, and lastly arrives at a total, harmonious resolution. If many of Claudel's characters have the priest in them, many also, after 1900, reflect the Mesa-Ysé union.

IX The Marriage

The next event is simple to describe. In April 1905 Claudel was back in France, where he stayed almost a year. In December he became engaged to Reine Sainte-Marie-Perrin of Lyons, daughter of the architect who designed the basilica of Notre Dame de Fourvière that overlooks the city. Three days after their marriage in March 1906 they were on the high seas, en route toward Claudel's third consular mission to China. The marriage did have a stabilizing function. And it does seem to have been somewhat arranged: Claudel may, at the age of thirty-seven, have felt it was now or never. It was a superb success. Five children graced their ever-changing hearths; many grandchildren were the joy of his retirement; and the rendering of his existence into something so calm and steady made of him a more tranquil listener of the universe's divine music.

His fortunate marriage and the increasing success of his two careers no doubt reduced the conflict-tensions that had been until 1906 so important to his creative forces. Counteracting elements still abounded: dissatisfaction at not having been a priest; memory of his past sins; recognition of his human failings; the imperfections he saw in the rest of the world; the feeling, despite success, that in terms of both careers he had opponents on account of his Catholicism. But the post-*Partage* works are clearly serener. Assuredness within his catholic-Catholic universe was substituted for losses in tensions as a force of inspiration. Prouhèze and Rodrigue of *Le Soulier de satin* fall in love; she calmly makes of her slipper (perhaps a reference to the possible shipboard incident that brought Claudel and "Ysé" together) an ex-voto to the Virgin Mary to assure her own spiritual purity. Rodrigue calmly accepts the effects of her decision if indeed he has not already arrived at the same conclusions she has already reached. The thorny rose is a recurrent and effective Claudelian symbol for carnal love; in fact, "Rose" was Ysé's real name.

X   The Rest of his Life and Work

Claudel's most important dramatic works written subsequent to *Partage* are the already-mentioned *Annonce faite à Marie* and *Soulier de satin,* plus the *Otage* trilogy, *L'Otage* (1908-1910; *The hostage*), *Le Pain dur* (1913-1914; *Stale bread*), *Le Père humilié* (1915-1916; *The Holy Father humiliated*). After *Cinq Grandes Odes* he wrote so much poetry, especially in short forms, that it seems unrepresentative to quote from any one poem on the subject of his life. The publication dates of the various collections are often rather misleading as to when a given poem in them was created. After *Art poétique* and until the end of the 1920's, publication dates of his prose are just as unrevealing. His prose, poetry, theater are similar thematically because his greatest concern—a re-presentation of a single universe under God with all its parts related or interrelated—is behind everything he wrote since his conversion. Their differences are the differences between genres and between the muses of the moment.

The year 1928 marks what is better called an expansion than a
turning point. He continued to write poetry, plays, "secular"
essays, but the greatest concern was elsewhere: In *J'aime la Bible*
(1949-1954) Claudel summarizes his contacts with the Old and
New Testaments. In that year he had been asked to write a preface to an edition of the *Revelation* of St. John: in French, *L'Apocalypse*. Since Christmas 1886 he had read and re-read the Bible,
but this was a new challenge. He buried himself even deeper in
the Scriptures, starting naturally with *Revelation*. In the end, he
never did write the asked-for preface. Instead, he produced the
five hundred page *Au milieu des vitraux de l'Apocalypse* (1928-
1932; *Among the stained-glass windows of the Apocalypse*), the
first of his several biblical commentaries. To date (1970), eight volumes (XIX-XXVI) subtitled *Commentaires et exégèses* have appeared in the *OEuvres complètes* with perhaps more to come.
Some of his other prose is not so secular; some of his commentaries
wander back to more secular themes. Since "exegesis" means critical biblical interpretation, some may hold that the term does not
apply to Claudel's written reactions to the Scriptures, which
seem more like stream-of-consciousness, save for the control represented by their author's anagogic frame of reference. Anagoge
in itself is not criticism, is not literature, but is a point of view
that determines other things. Furthermore, Claudel did not consider himself to be an exegete in any strict sense of the word.

After China Claudel went, in posts of ever-increasing importance, to Prague (1910-1911), Frankfort and Hamburg (1912-
1914), Rome (1915-1916), Rio de Janeiro (1917-1918), Copenhagen (1919-1921). Then he was elevated to Ambassador, serving in that rank in Tokyo (1921-1927), Washington (1927-1933),
Brussels (1933-1935). In 1927 he had bought (with money earned
and invested from his two careers) the château of Brangues
(Isère), in which village—ironically, for he detested Stendhal—
the prototype of Julien Sorel slew his ex-mistress. He lived peace-
fully there and in Paris from 1935, the year of his retirement, until
his death on February 23, 1955. Before the war he deplored Hitler, Mussolini, Stalin. At its onset he specifically deplored the
persecution of the Jews. During Vichy he accepted Pétain, dedi-
cating to him the poem "Paroles au maréchal" (1940; "Words to
the Marshall"; *Poèmes de guerre*). Its contents are not very different from the 1944 "Au général de Gaulle," appearing in the same

collection. Holding this to be two-faced overlooks Claudel's catholic-Catholic vision, or the overall worth of his work, or the fact that a similar viewpoint was held by the vast majority of his fellow-Frenchmen, not to mention the resurgent Pétainism of 1970 France and the insignificance of the Pétain problem as opposed to MacArthur's whitewash of the much more culpable Mikado. A good case could be made that he was a reactionary. But this matters little, given his stupendous appreciation of the unity of the universe, and his great success in enabling others to partake of his vision.

CHAPTER 2

Themes

A THEMATIC explanation may help not only neophytes but those fairly well launched into Claudel's works. There is so much primary material that some repetitions may be missed by many who have read a good deal of Claudel, either because they have not seen the forest for the trees or because, by an adverse stroke of fate, they have read the wrong works to make certain themes stand out as such. It goes without saying that recognition of a writer's themes is essential to knowing him and measuring him.

From the outset, one must realize that Claudel's prosody harks back to *poiema*, Greek for "poem" but also for "anything made," and to the verb *poiein*, "to poetize," "to make," "to do."[1] What then is not poetry? Thus, Claudel's themes cross his genres without exception, and indeed in this light, genres can be themes, as is shown immediately after these introductory paragraphs.

All of which is not to imply that thematizing Claudel is easy. Rather, it is difficult and nerveracking. No Claudelian thematic gloss will satisfy one and all. What may seem a theme to one critic may seem a subtheme or an aspect of a theme to another, or perhaps in no wise a theme. And the initial critic may miss some. These early years of Claudel criticism are difficult, groping ones, especially on the subject at hand.[2] Is *etiam peccata* an aspect or a subtheme of love, is love a subtheme of woman, or vice versa? Is the recurrent memory of the *Partage* incident a theme in its own right, or does it draw on themes like love, *etiam peccata*, woman? But such critical gropings must go on since they are the only route that can successfully encompass the *massif claudélien*. There will always be some confusion in this necessary approach, given Claudel's point of departure of the divine universal analogy, or the universal analogy under God. If everything is related, there are no hard and fast divisions between the themes.

Notwithstanding these reservations, I have grouped what seem to me Claudel's main themes under three headings. He had much to say of "Art"—his own and others! It is a mutual rallying point. Certain "Events" dominated his life and from them sprang many frequent subjects in his work. As a sometime philosopher or naturally as a fervent Catholic, he was much concerned with the "City of men" and often planned its outlines as he imagined his God would draw them. In some instances, certain themes are grouped side by side to aid the discussion of them, as in the example immediately following. Generally excluded for their supreme obviousness are some themes bound up with God, heaven, saints, prayer, the Bible, proselytizing.

A. ART

I His Own Art, Receptivity, the Poet's Role, the Universal Analogy

Claudel habitually referred to his own *Art poétique* (1900-1904), for good reason. This early series of essays shows very well the point of view that had dominated and was to dominate Claudel's whole life and works. There follow quotations from it so self-explanatory and succinct as to warrant relatively little extra comment and no paraphrasing.[3]

Man thought that all things at all times, with time's consent and fashioned by the same inspiration which measures his own development, elaborated a mystery which had absolutely to be discovered (V, 13).

... perhaps, nearer than stars and planets, all the moving, living things surrounding us give us ... sure signs and ... a vague explanation of the interior propulsion which makes our own life ours (14).

An immense and total hour is constantly being calculated ... (13).

To be is to create. All things in time listen, concert and compose. Physical forces and human wills encountering each other cooperate in the confection of the mosaic Instant (31).

There is a harmony, at each moment of total time (*la durée*) between all the parts of creation, from the Seraphim to the earthworm ... (110).

The Harmonic Cause or movement regulating the assembling of beings at a given moment of total time. That is Poetic Art. The new Logic, using the metaphor to express it (12).

The old Logic had the syllogism as its basic organ, but this one has the metaphor, the new word, the operation resulting from existence alone, joined to and simultaneous with two different things (35-36).

All things know each other either contiguously or complementarily (43).

... matter has two ordinary states, depending on whether it is establishing or maintaining its equilibrium. The first ... answers fairly well the words in our mind that have to do with conception and imagination. ... The second state is the attestation of the arrangement it has reached (51).

... that double beat of consciousness whose figures in this life are breathing, heart pulsations, the sharp and the dull (*l'aigu et le grave*), the shorts and the longs, the fundamental iamb of all language. ... The word ... is not only the sign of a certain state of our sensibility, it is the evaluation of the effort we had to dispense to form it, or rather to form ourselves in it. The poet, who has mastery over all words and whose art is to use them, is, by a clever disposition of the objects words represent, skilled at provoking within us a state of intelligence that is harmonious and intense, exact and strong (111).

Claudel's outlook was based on the supreme analogy linking earth to heaven. All other analogies spring from this one, as far as he was concerned. A tree, roots in the ground, branches lifting to the sky, was his favorite image of metaphoric language in general.[4] *Art poétique* treats at length the contribution to perception made by the senses, the intellect, and the conscience. Implying when not stating, the work sees the primary duty of the material universe as one of testimony, that is, to be represented, or *re*-presented, or simply presented in total time. The word-gifted poet, representing (in both senses) the existence he perceives, sings of creation as is his duty. Symbolism's universal analogy is essentially earthbound, as are ineffable, unattainable, impossible ideals. One senses that Symbolists sometimes looked on such a concept more as an approach to poetry than as a means to reaching truth in itself. On the other hand, Claudel believed in it fundamentally, not only as a way to evoke the nature of God and of created things, but as a revered divine truth. It is from this position that he melded the two meanings of catholic. For others, big C may be part of little c. For Claudel big or or little amounted to the same entity, the Catholic Church Triumphant.

One of the "others" was Baudelaire, whose influence on Claudel has already been referred to. To repeat, Baudelaire took many positions in his poetry, one of which was belief in the universal analogy. He did not gamble everything on this one concept, perhaps because of his rather weak belief in God and heaven during the years he wrote *Les Fleurs du mal.* Simply as a poet he would have made many similes. Being a poet who uses the universal analogy, he has in his work an astonishingly high proportion of simile-introducing words (like *comme* and *ainsi*). Influenced by this aspect of Baudelaire and doing his forerunner one better by in effect staking his all on it, Claudel is doubtless one of the greatest simile-makers in the history of poetry. Baudelaire is not far behind. Random page-openings in their poetry and in that of others is (unempirical) proof of this.

The "stomachic" Christian that Claudel was absorbed all existence as if it were food, consciously as well as unconsciously. The 1939 *Poème de guerre* "Ballade" provides one of the many conscious examples of this figure:

> My philosophers taught me there's no difference between yes and no.
> But one of my viscera, my stomach, can tell perfectly well what's good.

> Mes philosophes m'ont appris qu'il n'y a aucune différence entre oui et non.
> Mais je possède un certain viscère, l'estomac, qui sait parfaitement ce qui est bon (II, 255).

II Le Verset claudélien—
Components, Possible Sources, Construction

While it may seem arbitrary to treat the *verset* as a theme (rather than to relegate it to a section on style), Claudel's free verse lyric line is more than a prosodic phenomenon. It is deeply involved with his way of looking at Creation, and is therefore bound up with content, as well as with form. The *verset* is also a theme in that Claudel frequently, and in all his genres, took time out to explain painstakingly to his audience both its form and its content. As already noted, the receptivity of Symbolism and an intense conviction in a divine and harmonious universal analogy are important elements of the total inspiration. Claudel has just been quoted as relating respiration, heartbeat, and consciousness

to the "fundamental iamb of all language." Here iamb means
something unimportant coming before something important and
is independent of syllabic count. It is metaphoric, Pascalian,
something ordinary enough in poetry because the important is
usually climactic. There may be either one or more iambs to the
line. The last iamb of a line may, in terms of the whole line, form
the second or stressed half of a linear super-iamb, with all that
precedes it comprising the first half. An illustration follows in a
few pages.

Sometimes insufficient artistic self-restriction harmed Roman-
ticism. Symbolism accepted Romantic egocentricity, and couched
it in more universal terms that were still personal but not intimate
to the same degree. Claudel let himself follow Symbolism's more
limited lines. Definable components of the *verset claudélien* were
his trancelike receptivity, his primitivistic approach to the metaphor, his complete faith in *the* analogy, and his supreme poetic
sensitivity. Breathing and pulsating in harmony with the visible
and invisible universe, the poet re-presented it testimonially in
his poetic line. Thus the double cycle of the iamb is much more
than a poetic metaphor of only its author's breathing process. The
reader who already realizes the problems involved in attempting
to define lyricism pure and simple can perhaps sense—more than
define and measure—the qualities of Claudel's lyrical *verset*.

He often denied any great influence on him of the biblical
verse, claiming that he arrived at his own form independently.
Still, some critics see a biblical resonance in it, and others raise
also the possibility of the influence of Whitman, probably read
by Claudel in 1886. But his inimitability, or that of the *verset*, is
the real proof that the latter sprang more from Claudel's own
nature than from any conscious or unconscious attempt on his part
to copy other works. And while his earliest-known free verse,
the 1886 *Endormie*, was written at just the time when he might
have been especially susceptible to the double influence of Whitman and the Bible, it is more than likely that *L'Endormie* was
preceded by other free verse efforts that were destroyed, or have
not yet come to light. In a 1916 lecture-recital, Claudel explained
how his own free verse differed from that of others, in what way
it marked a reaction to traditional prosody, and that any question of influence should be directed more to French prose in general than to poetry:

You are not expecting me to enter into useless and fastidious explanations on the particular form I adopted from the moment I began to
write and which has the formal liberty of prose and which resembles
poetry because of certain laws of internal structure and of limits imposed on it by the blank space (*le blanc*). The distinction I personally
denote between myself and the various practitioners of free verse is
that they have tried to break the old line down and achieve more
flexibility, whereas all I have done is hand myself over to the traditional current of our French prose by substituting for a numerical and
artificial rhythm that of the word itself coming from our mouths and
lungs, interrupted and scanned by emotion and sentiment, and which
somehow is created in both the writer's and the spectator's hearts in a
series of intelligible movements (notes to *Accompagnements*; XVIII,
460).[5]

Almost a theme in themselves are such pronouncements on how
to act his plays, recite or understand his poetry, though of course
they are after the fact. And it is to be noted how they stem from
the need to explain his inimitable *verset*.

Although the main aspects of Claudel's line have to do with
the inspiration behind it, and although others have paid quite
enough attention already to its structure, this subject must be
gone into here. Sometimes one reads that the *verset* is a physiological as opposed to a psychological breath. This cannot be true.
Some *versets* are so long that it is impossible to emote them in a
single gasp. Some critics complain about lines like these from the
first *Tête d'or*:

> Si vous songez que vous êtes des hommes et que vous v-
> -Ous voyez empêtrés de ces vêtements d'esclaves, oh! cri-
> -Ez de rage . . . (Part II; VI, 157).

There is no use translating this. What may draw disapproval is
the "vous" (you) broken up as it is, and the first syllable of
"criez" (cry) gaining a stress it cannot have according to the
manuals. Not only has Tête d'or never read anything on pho-
netics, but he is excited and emoting outside of "calm" speech
patterns. Furthermore, the second "Ous" of "vous vous voyez"
would often be barely audible in rapid conversation (it would
be less so than the five letters that precede it, but even these are
hard to hear sometimes), and so Claudel most naturally contrived
to get them out of the position of stress that the end of a poetic
line usually exerts, even if unintentionally. Furthermore, Claudel

wanted to underline that it was the "vous" that Tête d'or was addressing. As for the abnormal breakup of the second word, evidently Claudel was after the imitative stridency of the syllable "cri-".

Of course, the French idea of iamb is quite different from the English. In regard to a long Pascalian paragraph (often fashioned on the Latin *perioda*), its iambic quality simply means that Pascal's most important statement comes last. One could just as well speak of Bossuet in this respect, since both he and Pascal worked with *périodes*; and, incidentally, early or late Claudel was consciously and/or unconsciously influenced by both these writers. In a paragraph by either of them, the less important precedes the more important, and in each part there may be sub-iambs, or sub-sub-iambs. Except that a single *verset* is infrequently of paragraph-length, the same considerations hold true for it. And because English and French word-orders are so similar, what is in question can be illustrated in translation:

> My God, take pity on these desirous waters!
> My God, you see I am not only mind, but water!
> take pity on these waters in me dying of thirst!
> And the mind is desirous, but water is the thing
> desired.

> Mon Dieu, ayez pitié de ces eaux désirantes!
> Mon Dieu, vous voyez que je ne suis pas seulement
> esprit, mais eau; ayez pitié de ces eaux en moi qui
> meurent de soif!
> Et l'esprit est désirant, mais l'eau est la chose
> désirée ("L'Esprit et l'eau," 1906; *Cinq Grandes Odes;*
> I, 82).

In a typical French sentence the thought groups of normal conversation are basically iambic and sub-iambic. Regular phonetic considerations, in effect, often help to determine the structure of a *verset*. In the first line, "My God" is unstressed, the rest is stressed. This is the basic iamb. But the stressed half can be divided into a sub-iamb: "Take pity," "on these desirous waters!" In the second line the first exclamation mark would seem to separate the unstressed from the stressed. The first subsidiary iamb of the stressed part is like that in the first line, but there is also a further breakdown. "... on these waters in me": what are they like? They are "dying of thirst."

III *Inspiration*

Claudel's broad interpretation of the word "poet" as a doer or maker extends to cosmic proportions themes that have at first glance only to do with poetry. Such is the theme of inspiration and creation. Claudel basically construed inspiration to be divine grace. For him, then, inspiration infiltrated into every aspect of life. Claudel's most common inspiration images are connected with water, music, night, blindness, woman. Water is a self-explanatory image, although it may be worth pointing out the advantage in French of the mer-mère (sea-mother) homonyms. Music: the orchestrated universe; God's silent trumpets; the divine melody there only for the heeding and the *Nec impedias musicam* (Do not hinder the music) from *Ecclesiasticus*. Night: silence, the moon and the stars. Blindness: freedom from visual detraction, permitting of a more fundamental and greater receptivity. Woman: God's message is love; the Beatrice role. Of course the inspiration enters through all the senses. Given the "fact" of synesthesia as propounded by Baudelaire in "Correspondances" plus the general Symbolist emphasis on the senses, sensory paradoxes are understandably frequent in Claudel; just as understandably, blindness paradoxes predominate. Woman as theme is complex enough for a separate entry.

Pertinent here is the already-cited phenomenon of his play versions. Habitually he wrote in a state of inspired receptivity and rewrote mainly only to provide a clean copy for the typesetter. He cannot be criticized, for after all his system worked. The transitoriness or non-recurrent aspect of his moments of writing must have meant that to an extent his own texts were subsequently unrecognizable to their own creator. Later, under reason's cold light, he naturally was wont to change so much in a given work as to make it genuinely distinct from its previous version.

IV *Animus and Anima*

Animus is the earth, Anima heaven. He is the body, she the soul. Animus is man, Anima woman, he everyday life, she the divine light that comes into it. One is the poet, whose inspiration is the other. Several other like pairings are readily conceivable. The two figures are named in Claudel's "Parabole d'Animus et

42   PAUL CLAUDEL

d'Anima," which forms part of the larger essay "Réflexions et propositions sur le vers français" (1925; *Positions et propositions I*). They serve many themes but merit an existence of their own because Claudel often thought in terms of Animus and Anima as he wrote his duets. So it is when the lovers Prouhèze and Rodrigue converse (*Le Soulier de satin* [1919-1924]), and when Azarias—the archangel Raphael—or Sara speak to the latter's father-in-law Tobie (*L'Histoire de Tobie et de Sara* [1938]). Named first in the 1925 "Parabole," later specifically referred to a number of times, Animus and Anima explain a concept or series of concepts that clearly precede their "creation" in the mid-twenties.

V   Advantages of Christian Art

Allied with Claudel's belief in the divine nature of creation and inspiration was his conviction that the Christian artist, profiting from these things, had a natural advantage. Claudel saw him as working from within where grace had reached, thus rendering the artist's whole being germane to what he represented. On the other hand, the "pagan" artist worked from without. Thomas Aquinas' *Summas* may have helped crystallize this viewpoint, expressed time and time again in all the genres.

VI   Humor and or Laughter

Fowler breaks up humor in general into humor, wit, satire, sarcasm, invective, irony, cynicism, the sardonic.[6] The second *Cahier Paul Claudel*[7] is subtitled *Le Rire de Paul Claudel* (*Paul Claudel's laughter*). A book, then, has already been written on the humor in his life and works; others could be. The cited *Cahier* also stresses a sort of humor not plotted by Fowler, springing from sheer joy or jubilation in the face of what Claudel looked on as a wondrous universe. This is positive humor. The other sorts are more chastizing and negative. Positive or negative, all of Claudel's humor evidently has very much to do with the actual state of the world as compared to the state Claudel thought God wanted it to be in.

VII   Life and Influences

Claudel was frequently queried about his life and about influences in his work. Humanly, he had the same curiosities himself, about himself. His replies to others or to his own sense of curiosity constitute an important part of his work and are in effect an all-pervasive theme of his work.

VIII *Poetic Art and Literary Criticism*

Claudel wrote much on language as well as on traditional and non-traditional poetry. Of course he had a good deal to say specifically about certain poets, some of whom, because of his special conception of poetry, are not poets in the generally accepted sense. Those he was drawn to often resemble him in some ways. Some of these no doubt influenced him, while with others it is more a question of kindred spirits.

The Greek and Roman classics he most often referred to are Pindar, Homer, Aeschylus, Horace, Virgil, Seneca. Saint Thomas Aquinas and Saint Augustine are much present, but not for literary reasons. Non-French *littérateurs* of the living tongues who recur in his writings the most are Dante, Shakespeare, Dostoevsky, Poe, Coventry Patmore. The French writers most dwelt on are Racine, Bossuet, Chateaubriand, Hugo, Baudelaire, Rimbaud, Verlaine, Mallarmé; French-language contemporaries receiving more than minimal treatment are Gide, Jammes, André Suarès, Saint-John Perse, Charles-Louis Philippe, Aragon, Romain Rolland, Ramuz, Giraudoux.

IX *Painting*

Painting always interested him, above all during his ambassadorship to Belgium when of course he had access to many Flemish collections. One entire prose work, *L'OEil écoute* (1934-1945; *The eye listens*), is devoted mainly to art commentaries, most of them on the Dutch masters. And just as one part of that work is entitled "Sur la musique," anywhere in his other books may one find a sudden digression on painting or on a painter.

X *Music*

There is the already-discussed "divine music." In many other ways, Claudel was deeply involved with music. His connections with Symbolism alone dictated involvement with his own words' musicality, and there was also Symbolist music—that of Berlioz, Wagner, and others. But in general, religious and profane music drew his attention, attention that was obliged to be technical when he wrote libretti and evaluated the program music composed for his plays.

XI Dance and Puppetry

The onstage associations between human motions and emotions meant that from the outset Claudel was interested in the dance. Also, there is its relation to music. His three sojourns in China added another stratum of influence as did, though more strongly still, his ambassadorship to Japan. He wrote on puppetry and on such dramatic forms as the No and the Kabuki, used their and other oriental dance techniques in his dramatic works, and choreographed oriental ballets and puppet acts.

XII Sculpture

His keen awareness of this plastic art began with his early knowledge of Parnassian poetry and of course grew when his sister Camille developed into a supremely gifted sculptress. Because of her liaison with Rodin, the latter's work too became most familiar to Claudel. Religious statuary also drew his comments.

XIII Architecture and Glassmaking

These sister themes awoke in him long before his marriage to an architect's daughter. One source of his interest was the medieval period—which he much admired—whose churches and cathedrals were its greatest artistic manifestations. Another source was the simple fact of the houses raised to God in any age. Third, the assymetric unity of a gothic building served him as a good symbol of all creation, with God as the master architect. Lastly, architecture was bound to draw his attention as an aspect of modernity the eyes can not ignore.

XIV Cinema, Radio, Photography

These comparatively recent arts attracted Claudel for their newness and also because they were susceptible of being drawn into his artistic schemes. Thus he wrote about them in a general way. But in addition he used cinematographic techniques in some of his later plays, wrote radio plays, and composed commentaries to photographic material.

B. *EVENTS*

Claudel was an apocalyptic Christian from 1886 on. As such, he tended to read fate into the striking occurrences of his life, especially if they were touched with coincidence. The key events are referred to often throughout his work. Another sort of event played another sort of role: His given location at a given moment influenced him in deducible ways. The philosophic question of time and space is too complicated for these pages,[8] but the areas to which he was posted played their roles in his life and appear as themes in his work.

I *Christmas*

Claudel found his faith on Christmas, 1886, and formally converted four years later to the day. Christmas in itself was important to him as a Christian. He read deeply into the lives of the saints. Two of these, Lydwina of Schiedam and Colette of Corbie, had special associations with Christmas. His good friend Francis Jammes' second child was born on Christmas Day. A direct proof of the inspirational value of the Day of the Nativity is found in the number of smaller pieces bearing that completion date. One interpretation of Claudel is that he was "born" on Christmas Day, that he is a Nativity Christian.[9]

II *Death*

As it has been noted, Claudel returned to Villeneuve at the age of thirteen and literally witnessed the death from cancer of his grandfather. Already mentioned also is the fact that during his atheistic or agnostic period he toyed with the idea of suicide. Above and beyond this detail, the four-year period represented to him a time of spiritual death. Awe of death, as distinct from preoccupation with it, diminished proportionately as his philosophic doubts waned, as his serenity in his faith waxed. Christ's death and resurrection naturally demanded his attention; another way to consider Claudel is as an Easter Christian, who rose from spiritual death to spiritual life.[10]

III Love

To be repeated in a later paragraph of this chapter is the fact that Claudel was an extremely "male" writer to the point of being an antifeminist. Love therefore was seen by him with a masculine basis. What role love played in his early life is not clear. Some see *Partage*-like themes in his pre-1900 work. If they are there, they are disoriented, more in the nature of thoughts than ideas. But before or after that date *God's* love is the message[11]; earthly love, platonic or carnal, is a symbol of it in the divine scheme of things, which scheme is designed to inspire in humans love of the Deity and love among themselves insofar as they are the Deity's creatures. Through Claudel's male optic, this amounts to the Beatrice theme. It works the other way too, but the reverse direction—literature in general being masculine—has no special name. Such a conception of love is both theory and theme in Claudel.

IV ETIAM PECCATA

The catalyst for Claudel's insistence on this Saint Augustine quotation—sins also serve the divine purpose—would seem to be *the* great sin of his life. However, *Le Repos du septième jour*, written four years before the experience, contains these words: "Evil is in the world like a slave bringing up water" (VIII, 231). One can say that in general the problem of the existence of sin in a universe created by a good God perturbed Claudel as it must most of those who believe in a benevolent Deity. His special sin brought the problem closer to home; he now felt he had to solve it, not just note its existence. Apocalyptically, he believed strongly that God's hand was mysteriously involved. As mentioned before, the other epigraph of *Le Soulier de satin* (besides *etiam peccata*) is "God writes straight with crooked lines." Thus the profane mystery that puzzled Claudel before his second China tour, tortured him during it, was subsequently elevated to the rank of a religious mystery—something one does not understand but which in all certainty *is*. Especially in his plays, he often seemed to regard sin-like deeds with indulgence. This attitude was no doubt ascribable to both conscious and unconscious reasons, though also his characters act on symbolic levels of value. Later in life, his viewpoint changed somewhat. Sin might serve a divine end, but still the potential sinner has a conscience. That is, *etiam peccata* eventually assumed in his work more of a confessional savor.

V *Woman*

This complex theme is of course related to many others, such as family, love, *etiam peccata*, and inspiration. Three female figures are primarily responsible for the great importance of Woman in Claudel's work: the Virgin Mary, for understandable reasons; "Ysé"; the womanly personification of divine wisdom in the *Proverbs* passage he read on the fateful Christmas Day of 1886. One could say that his encounter with the Virgin Mary occurred on the same day. The *mer-mère* homonym and the idea of "Holy Mother Church" also reinforced the general theme. The real story behind *Partage de midi* is often reflected in Claudel's work. It could be considered that there exists a *Partage* theme in its own right, or that references to the incident represent a combination of the themes of Woman and *etiam peccata*.

VI *Fate*

This is one fashion of considering certain things already said and to be said. Claudel and "Ysé" were star-crossed lovers (*amants stellaires*). Claudel was *meant* to go to Notre Dame on the day he did, *meant* to open the Bible later to certain passages. His idea of the fate of his own life was transferred to the imaginative aspects of his work. Divine intervention is part of the greater concept of epiphany, which is gone into differently in the third section of this chapter.

VII *Vocation and Separation*

Under this classification one cannot overlook Claudel's vocation as a poet: "The general idea of my life and vocation . . . is a great desire and a great movement toward divine joy and the attempt to link the whole world to it . . ." ("Préface à Jacques Madaule" [1930], *Accompagnements*, XVIII, 327). Nor can one dismiss consular and diplomatic work, to which he brought fully

sufficient abilities. But of course the vocation most important to
Claudel was the one denied him in 1900, that of being a monk or
a priest. Until the refusal, his yearning was one of hope; afterward, it was one of resignation. Claudel's deep sadness on this
count is something with which a reader easily sympathizes. Hand
in hand with vocation goes separation, in the sense that a priest
is "not of this century." Claudel's solitary nature and his necessary solitude as a writer extended the idea of separation beyond
a purely religious context.

VIII *Conflicts*

Like "fate," this category invades and is invaded by the others.
Yet it is useful to point out that until serenity set in during the
late 1920's, Claudel lived a life of conflicts or tensions that are
abundantly reflected in his work. And perhaps even in his last
period the anagogic war he waged on biblical literalism
amounted to a tension. Vocation-nonvocation, poet-priest, dis-
belief-belief, pessimism-optimism: these are some conflicts or tensions and there are numerous others.

IX *Diatribes*

This could also fall under the third broad category, "City of
men." Still, the large majority of his diatribes amount to one long
attack against a single happening and the causes thereof, his fall
from faith in 1882 just at the time he entered Louis-le-Grand.
No matter the genre or subject, at any moment a stream-of-consciousness association was liable to set him inveighing against
any conceivable agent of his descent to the free-thinking materialistic ambience that had let what happened to him happen.
Since he was personally responsible to a degree, his harangues
may have helped relieve the resultant guilt pangs, but this possibility is not consciously present in his countless attacks against
Luther, Calvin, Voltaire, Kant, Goethe, Nietzsche, Poe, Baudelaire,
Mallarmé, Wagner, Balzac, Descartes, Renan, Zola, Flaubert,
Darwin, Huxley, Robespierre, Cousin and the rest of the "dia-
bolic" horde.

It would be making a philosopher out of a poet—trying to establish a logical development where it is only a question of successive *états d'âme*—to draw far-reaching conclusions from the

other objects of his invectives. He replied in kind to hostile criticism of his life and work. He hated venomously any country that
fought his own, at least for the time it took to write many a short
piece. The Académie française took its good time receiving him,
and this found acid echoes in his work. Education and the University of Paris were special bugbears. Not only had they fostered
the atmosphere that brought on his fall, but they created aca-
demic critics approving only traditional literary forms, gramma-
rians accepting nothing new in language. Claudel's disgust at
Gide's homosexuality and his belief in his own God-involved type
of literature made Proust (who was a silent admirer of his) a
natural target over and over again. "Enemies" of the Church—
Spanish Loyalists, modernists, Combes, Maurras (who was not
a believer)—frequently drew his fire.

X   *Evolution*

To Claudel evolution was the unfolding of all creation under
the impulsion of the harmonic and divine primary cause. It is
relatable to his conception of the universal analogy, of fate, of
epiphany. As such an unfolding, evolution takes priority over
everything except the divine prime mover; human society, the
city of men, can thus be held to be more an aspect of it than the
other way round. In a sense, Claudel looked on evolution as a
contradiction in terms. If time is one (in terms of the universal
analogy), and if evolution is a phenomenon taking place in successive or multiple time, then it simply contradicts itself. But
there was something very personal and defensive in his preoccupation. Actually, he was reacting against the "godless" Darwinism
of the 1882 atmosphere he so anathemetized. He did not arrive
at a formal rebuttal until the early 1930's, through a symbol based
on the Hindi word for nature. "La Légende de Prâkriti" appeared
in the December 1933 issue of the *Nouvelle Revue Française*
(presumably it was written shortly before):

Prâkriti is not a sort of imminent goddess attending as if in a dream
to the vast diversity of existing things by an indefinite and ever more
detailed series of buddings and splittings, by an irrepressible turning
this way and that, but an artist answering the order for a play on a
set topic by constructing a theater, starting up all sorts of workshops
and forming a swarm of actors, each one with his little abilities in his
time and place (reprinted in *Figures et paraboles*, V, 213).

From then on Prâkriti often cropped up in his writings, although this concept of ever-continuing creation was nothing new to Claudel. Thirty years before, in *Art poétique,* he had written that "the cause is never the same, but the operation of an accumulating sum. . . . All movement . . . is *from* a point, and not *to* a point" (V, 38). Also:

Things, not unaided in their creation, are bound together by a mutual obligation. This obligation, purely physical and *formal* (in the plastic sense) in animal, is moral in free man. His conscience tells him whether he has or has not acted contrary to his nature or the design set down for him (96-97).

Claudel, Bergson, Proust. . . . Although contingencies can be manipulated to "prove" the contrary, most believe that Proust owes no debt to Bergson. Far off in China, Claudel read the latter's *Evolution créatrice* after having written *Art poétique.* It was pure and simple *Zeitgeist,* as his letters of the period show he realized. This additional coincidence furthermore would seem to substantiate that Proust too arrived independently at his conclusions. All three, after all, were refugees from Scientism.

XI   *Places in the World*

Claudel had four long missions in the Far East, three of them in China, one in Japan. The Oriental aspects of his work are too complex and broad to begin to enumerate them here. Most of them, though, are immediately recognizable as such. The traditional and close-to-nature Far East he knew was bound to please him. Of a different ilk were his two assignments to America, where he spent a total of eight years as opposed to the eighteen in China and Japan. By or during his second and longer stay he had started off on special artistic routes upon which America could make less of an impression than would have been the case before. Basically, the United States went against his grain, at least during his earlier stay; this is understandable, in the light of his reasons for liking the Far East. Contrariwise, America was a real symbol of the new way of the world—which he in general ultimately came to accept—and as Claudel grew older, more removed from his own "grain" and more attached to symbols, his view of it mellowed.

Almost chemical reactions put America and the Far East in a

special place in Claudel's writings. But he was an explicator of all things, all places. Naturally his own France was a frequent subject of explication, to his fellow Frenchmen as well as others. Amounting to a theme in his work, then, is Claudel's great preoccupation with explaining to the whole wide world the localities where he had been.

XII *Rimbaud*

Rimbaud crops up frequently in Claudel's writings.[12] Rimbaud the trader, the traveler, the seer, the man touched with grace, the man in other ways as well comparable to Claudel. There is of course the initial debt. Later, Claudel learned more about the life of the other poet and thus there are two layers in his work's Rimbaud-figures. First, the real debt of the influence of *Une Saison en enfer* and *Illuminations*. Second, the anecdotal Rimbaud, who in many ways resembled the anecdotal Claudel.

C. *CITY of MEN*[13]

As becomes more apparent, the more the various themes are presented, any one of the three categories—"Art," "Events," "City of Men"—is effectively a sort of coda to the others. Claudel's vision of creation's basic unity makes it impossible to establish isolated rallying points. Some critics see Proust bed-bound for most of his creative life: There are those who glue Claudel to a prayer stool in a Lady chapel. But that robust Christian lived a full life and was quite concerned how life in general should be lived. I have not yet treated his views on the duties of the individual as an individual, and also as a component of all the groups from the family to the world community. He thought as a Catholic in such domains, which at first consideration lays a barrier between much of his social thought and the non-Catholic. In many instances, a useful way to lift the barrier is to desacralize his sacral ideas. To cite an example, of course Claudel saw the ideal family unit as existing on a sacral or God-fearing plane, but such "God-fearingness" could be subtracted to make this position more palatable or reasonable to those not of his religious persuasion. While Claudel himself never used the word desacralization (and really it has not yet worked itself into many dictionaries, if it will ever do so), on occasion he favored a mental attitude that was much like it.

I Roles of Things, People, etc.

This category is a catchall. Claudel's predilection for explicating places in the world was part of his general tendency to pause to explain the role of anything or anybody—stones, pigs, professions—in the divine scheme of things.

II The Family

Of course there is women's inspirational role, already touched on. Claudel was for a close-knit, patriarchal family group. He was almost exclusively anti-femininist. For him man was the ambassador away from the family hearth. In this function, man gained a certain sort of wisdom but woman, closer to life's basics, had her own sort that was of great help to her family.

III Ownership, pro-STATUS QUO

By dictionary definition, Claudel was indubitably a reactionary. However, in the light of the total scheme of things, or from a sacral viewpoint of existence, he was far from it. He looked on ownership as trusteeship of God's belongings. He believed that the spirituality of such a trusteeship operates, or should operate, a check on the worldly "owner," keeping him from being a crass materialist in regard to the things he only apparently possesses, keeping him from "looking after" more than he can look after or should look after. Revolution and unstable conditions could damage the goods, so to speak, and should be avoided if possible. This orientation goes a long way to explaining why Claudel, who in 1939 deplored Hitler and the persecution of the Jews, could two years later accept Pétain, the man who gave to France the less revolutionary motto of "Work, Family, Country." Also why he could, at the war's end, just as easily acclaim de Gaulle. In another light altogether, it has already been pointed out that despite Claudel's references to a partly peasant family tree, he descended on the whole from bourgeois forebears and was a solid middleclass individual himself.

IV Politics, Personal Relationships

How seriously he did so is open to question, but Claudel often propounded the idea of a religious monarchy, which position for a while made him approve of the *Action Française,* though the areligiosity of its leader Charles Maurras eventually changed him into an ardent detractor. What he missed in post-monarchic systems was the more intimate relationships that he saw were possible between all men—not necessarily probable—under a monarchy. At the same time he was a realist, and also he accepted, albeit often begrudgingly, the present state of things as being an unfathomable manifestation of God's will. But even though he accepted, he did what he could to "correct" the situation, in physical deed and in writing. At the same time, his public position forced him to veil his political thoughts more than he would otherwise have done. This external consideration indicates that the reader-spectator can rightly hyperbolize the abundant political subtleties in Claudel's work. Claudel was not fond of most central governmental controls, but though not liking them, he was incapable of suggesting workable substitutes.

V *Justice*

For Claudel the word sparkled with many facets, one more in fact since he was French: Where the King James version of the Bible has "uprighteousness," French Bibles often have *justice.* He considered there were two types of justice among men, the negative one of the Ten Commandments, and the open or positive justice of charity.[14] Negative justice maintains the state of things, but the way to keep up inter-human dealings is charity—we owe everything to everyone. This latter variety of justice abounds in his work in many forms, from prayer, pilgrimage, and mystical suffering to the direct action of the good deed. One cannot fail to notice the existentialist overtones of charity so conceived. In a way, it provides another conflict in his work: between the placidity of his complete acceptance of his God and the anguish in the face of the uncharted nature of the charitable course through life that the same God prescribes for all men.

VI *Epiphany, the New Jerusalem*

A member of any proselytizing faith would want the whole world to participate in that religion. If Claudel sometimes envisioned such a universal "orchestra," it is doubtful that he thought its realization imminent. But there was the far-distant future in which, generally, Claudel had more trust that his dream would come to be. In this respect, his overall position was like that of Alfred de Vigny in his *Destinées*.

Epiphany, or manifestation of God's will on earth. At the beginning of his life Claudel detested depersonalization, mechanization, industrialization. Enough clues have already been provided to suggest why this was so. Later, he came to see advantages in material "progress." For example, in the last half of his life he could bring himself to write essays in praise of such modern things as motorcycles and airplanes. The diametrical shift was not entire, but general. Though often harking back rather wistfully to the *ancien régime* and disliking many of the fruits of the French Revolution, Claudel, all things considered, admitted the necessity of the events in 1789, admitted even that the divine monarchy he dreamed of had seen little reflection before that date. In many ways, even, France had *improved* by the change. His political breed would be unrecognizable to American egalitarian society. It would be more identifiable in England as something like a radical conservatism (for slow and reasonable change). He demonstrated against Combism, but could not more publicly say he was hostile to the government he served faithfully and well for over forty years. Thus Claudel, reactionary in essence or from an American liberal point of view, was a "practicing" *républicain*, and cheerful enough about it. There was no vast increase in church-going over his lifetime, but those who did believe, including the priesthood, consolidated their forces and their knowledge of their own faith. This religious resurgence was observed (often from afar) by Claudel and gave him heart.[15] He now saw no great hindrance to the achievement of God's will on earth, at least none such as he had witnessed in the France of his youth. One can read into his relative approval of the present an optimism in regard to the future. Epiphanally, he saw improvement and hoped for more.

Claudel's respect for Jewry stemmed from considering it as his God's first chosen people. This, Christianity could never take away from it. But with Christianity God's new chosen city moved west, and moved west first. Claudel often intimated that either France or the whole of Europe was a New Jerusalem, from either of which missionaries traveled to the whole world, in either of which saints prayed for the fate of all humanity, and whence useful ideas—practical as well as spiritual—emanated.

Combining his epiphanal thoughts with these considerations brings one full cycle back to the universal analogy, of a world much more conscious of being one, of a new unified Jerusalem dedicated to manifesting God's love, a dream he believed foretold the future. This vision is easily desacralized.

CHAPTER 3

Theater

IN THE original or in translation, Claudel's theater is naturally his most accessible genre. Which is his best or most important genre will be difficult to answer when enough time has passed to try to do so. An absolute position now would be suspect both because of Claudel's closeness and because of his huge production. After all, some critics hold that the same two factors still prevent a proper evaluation of Victor Hugo, who predates Claudel by two full generations.

At the present time, Claudel's theater *seems* to be the best and most important, as is evidenced by the attention paid it at the expense of his other genres in general anthologies and literary histories. But this no doubt returns one to the fact of its approachability. Even Jacques Madaule, the most prominent expert on Claudel's theater, goes no further than saying that it is probably the main part of his work, "but that is not completely sure."[1]

Unfairly, although Claudel the *poietes* would not have looked upon it as unfair, externals tend to distract from an attempt to know his plays for their individual ideas and artistic merits. Apart from reaction one way or the other to their religious or general orientation, the contemporary reader-spectator still brings to the task the excess baggage of acquaintance with Claudel's life and times. Also clouding the issue when one has before one a given play by Claudel is familiarity with his other works, especially further theatrical versions of the same basic plot. Most of these externals are normal stumbling blocks to the appreciation of an entire opus, which only time will dispel. None of them can be considered Claudel's "fault," save perhaps the last, which is ascribable in part to his usual manner of composition: To repeat, his custom of writing only during a brief period each day and his habit of not rereading or recomposing the results except in making a clean copy for the printer are no doubt to some extent behind the need he felt to create independent versions of so many basic plots.

All the same, Claudel's works should be viewed dually, on their own terms exclusively and in terms of anything else that helps to explain more about them.[2] Since much of the external evidence is relegated to the two preceding chapters, the three genre chapters, this one and the two following, are freer to deal with the internal. However, much would be lost if I did not at all directly relate individual plays to Claudel's spiritual and artistic development, when it seems appropriate.

With Claudel's theater in mind, Jacques Madaule divides Claudel's literary career into three chronological groups that are inarguably correct.[3] He calls them respectively "L'Invasion de la lumière," "Partage de midi," "La Saison du dépouillement." The first is from 1886 through 1900; the "invasion of light" of course refers to Claudel's conversion and carries him up to the point beyond which, had his vocation not been refused, he would have completely abandoned literature. The second, referring to the 1905 play, extends from its composition through 1925 and the completion of *Le Soulier de satin*. The final period, the "season of divestment," lasts from then until his death in 1955. Claudel's plays are presented here according to Madaule's three break-downs. Contrary to his order of presentation, strict chronology is adhered to within each period. What this loses in back to back comparisons of versions, it more than gains in following closely Claudel's development as a dramatist and, thereby, the distinctive quality of each play in its chronological turn.

A.   FIRST PERIOD 1888-1900

L'Endormie (1886[4]); *Une Mort prématurée* or *Fragment d'un drame* (1888); *Tête d'or,* 1st v. (1889); *La Ville,* 1st v. (1890); *La Jeune Fille Violaine,* 1st v. (1892-1893); *Agamemnon* (1892-1894); *L'Echange,* 1st v. (1893-1894); *Tête d'or,* 2nd v. (1894); *Le Repos du septième jour* (1895-1896); *La Ville,* 2nd v. (1897); *La Jeune Fille Violaine,* 2nd v. (1898-1900).

I   L'ENDORMIE, UNE MORT PREMATUREE

The first is a one-acter, the second only a fragment of a full play the rest of which, for personal reasons, Claudel destroyed.

They are mainly of historical interest only. *L'Endormie*, a classical rhapsody complete with prancing fauns, suggests still one more influence on Claudel's *verset*, the ancient dithyramb. *Une Mort prématurée* reveals suicidal, parricidal, incestuous acts or tendencies in one or the other of the two male characters and is thus of autobiographical interest: Claudel's pre-conversion unhappiness and leaning toward violence had not been completely and miraculously expunged by the events of Christmas Day 1886. Both of these dramatic efforts are lyrical, the distinction between them and what was to follow being one of quality.

II   TETE D'OR, 1st v.

Claudel's oldest extant full-length play is the first *Tête d'or*. Its forceful hero Simon Agnel acquires the nickname of the title because of his blond locks. The sickly anti-hero Cébès is clearly the other side of the coin. The play opens on a deserted field at winter's end. The area is foggy, stormy, poor-soiled, agricultural. Simon Agnel is in the background burying his dead mistress. In the foreground, Cébès—who has not yet seen him—monologs on the subject of his own René-like wretchedness:

Here I am,
Imbecilic, ignorant
New man before unknown things
And I turn my face toward the Year and the rainy ark, and my heart is full of ennui!
I know nothing and I am helpless. What can I say, or do? How can I use these trailing hands, these feet leading me along like dreams?[5]

Finally, this poet of weakness becomes aware of Simon Agnel.
The latter had left the region some time previously, accompanied by the woman he is now burying in her native soil. Simon had led a strong and adventurous life away from home though he too was and is possessed with uncertainty. "Hope," he says, "in the repose that comes after one's eyes are closed" (I; VI, 82). Cébès senses in him the conqueror and, since conquerors need the conquered, he kneels down before Simon, then leaves. Alone, Simon soliloquizes on his own indecision:

—Oh . . . Night, mother!
Crush me or stop up my eyes with earth!

Mother, why did you split the clay that held my eyelids together?
Mother, I'm alone! Mother, why do you force me to live?

How much better it would be for me if in the East tomorrow the
wet earth didn't turn red! Oh good one, become thick with me once
more!

I'm helpless! see me, your child!

And you, oh Earth, I feel you with my whole body!

Maternal Night! Earth! (90)

Simon and Cébès are certainly one and the same. One is reminded
of the two male characters in *Une Mort prématurée*.

As if *Tête d'or* were an opera, or a play by Maeterlinck, one
has to lend goodwill and application to the job of telling why
Act II opens far from the field, in the great hall of an indeterminate Palace, what the moribund Cébès is doing there, and why
the Emperor's followers are all sound asleep. The army is off
fighting for the kingdom's survival. Its commanding general Tête
d'or sends word of victory. The Princess arrives to comfort
Cébès, whom she has been attending, then leaves. Eventually the
victorious Simon appears, witnesses Cébès' death, then slays the
Emperor before the cringing courtiers, whose being asleep at the
act's beginning was a symbol of their present cowardice, of Gethsemane, of the miserable epoch described as follows by the third
watchman, one of five individuals who had managed to keep their
eyes open from the onset of the act:

—What's happened, Our sky's become cloudy.

Like fog, when the shopkeepers at noon squint into their tills,

It suddenly felt very peaceful here.

Ah! the pleasures, the poor joys, chatting and eating together under
the trees, and the sight of our companion with red cheeks and black
hair, the feminine woman,

All these things have lost their savor! (96)

So actually there was little worth rescuing. The Princess arrives;
her father had summoned her before Simon's appearance. Tears,
recriminations, but of a strong and heroic nature. Nevertheless,
she is obviously to be disinherited by Tête d'or. The new King
says:

... you know what I am and what I want.

Living men! I seem to come

As someone requesting something for nothing.

However, don't refuse what I want, which is Everything! (148)

Simon Agnel goes on to the promising if enigmatic future. So clearly a symbol of the adolescent who will not be repressed or depressed, this second Alexander prevails over the contrary forces of youth, those of surrender; Cébès, youth's alter ego, is dead. The vastness of Tête d'or's crime does not imply radical revolt: Simon, after all, is a general. The phenomenon is more personal than political or social. If anything, the Emperor was too lax.

Act III is set at the "frontiers of Europe." The new King has tried to conquer the whole world, but in this spot he meets defeat for himself, although his cry at the time when he is mortally wounded turns the tide: He had subjugated all Europe, and perhaps now his troops will dominate Asia. Symbolically, then, all life has been vanquished, but at what cost? The Princess now reduced to begging, has trailed after the army. On a mountain promontory an anarchic deserter robs her, then literally crucifies her to a tree; before he leaves, she tells him that he has "slain the woman who will never be found again" (184). Later, the dying Tête d'or is hoisted to the same spot, though no one sees the Princess. He momentarily revives to state to his lieutenants his lack of belief in a hereafter, then:

I swear it before you and I attest to the black Night . . .
Nothing. And it doesn't matter. What do I care about the Past
Which is really the whole song . . . nothing but a word!
And, logically, I should care just as little about the Future! However,
I could say that I'm leaving the theater still unsated.
Naked I go into death but with a
Living desire!
—But life, in the strongest bull as in the frailest flower, blown out!
—Why should we want to keep our eyes open
Against sleep's eternal fatigue? (211)

On his orders he is left alone. He and the Princess discover each other. With his last strength he rises to tear the nails from the tree, freeing her. She had once inspired Cébès. Now the Princess uplifts the King, who says to her: "O Grace with pierced hands!/ Gentle as the dying sun!/ . . . /The sight of you casts a spell on me, Benediction!/ . . . /I hope! I hope! I aspire!/You can't break into my firm soul with your woman's hands . . ." (220, 222-3). Just

before he dies, some of his men reappear. He tells them to crown
the Princess. He dies; they crown her; she dies.

Even some of Claudel's better subsequent plays will not be
treated as lengthily. Merely because it is his first full-length
drama, *Tête d'or* deserves both fanfare and considerable examination, not to speak of its many touches of genius. The 1889 *Tête
d'or* has only to be compared with Chauteaubriand's *René* to
show its simplest level of meaning. The latter work is a symbol
of an attitude more psychophilosophical, that is, more universal,
than Romantic. *Tête d'or* certainly transposes the same attitude
to a much more removed plane of symbols. Since both works tell
a similar story and reach comparable resolutions, *René* would
seem to be an effective measure of *Tête d'or*'s quality. The latter
work presents a more believable interpretation of the common
subject, that is, the nature of adolescence emerging into manhood.
This nature is dual, alternating between insipid and forceful, ad-
jectives highly descriptive of Cébès and Simon Agnel respectively. There is also something richly persuasive about its lyrical
free verse, whose lengths parallel the mental meanders of both the
hero and the anti-hero. One can also surmise, although artistically
this is irrelevant, that *Tête d'or*'s creator was closer to the general
thoughts and feelings concerned than was *René*'s. The couched
didacticism of *Tête d'or* is probably more palatable than the
straight moral tale of *René*, though this judgment may be arbitrary. The play seems to say: Strong-willedness is better than
weak-willedness, because the latter ends in nothing; there *is*
something else, a hereafter, not ill-defined but simply not defined
in the play. The Princess certainly inspires, but her message is
obscure. Is she a representative of womankind, of grace, of Religion, of the Church, of the Virgin Mary? One can draw "biblical"
conclusions from internal evidence alone: Most outstanding are
the Gethsemane and crucifixion connotations.

René is of course clearer than *Tête d'or*. This means nothing in
itself. Perhaps indeed, *Tête d'or*'s vagueness within each act is
salutary. The author's intentions do eventually affect his audience
or readers, in both the realms of *états d'âme* and ideas. Perhaps,
even, *René* is too lucid, too essay-like. Where *Tête d'or* may suffer
more from lack of clarity is the already-mentioned pair of ellipses
between acts. Consecutiveness of action does not make a play and
can even destroy the spirit of theater, though if the playwright

adopts it generally as a means to something else he should probably adhere to it. *Tête d'or*'s three settings are vastly different in time and place; an attempt to be like Wagner or Maeterlinck? Why, if the first and second acts occur in an unnamed countryside and an indeterminate kingdom respectively, does the third take place in a better-indicated locale, the outskirts of Europe? How did Cébès get to the Palace, the Princess to the Caucasus? And if one says the artist has his rights, then in these instances the author practiced them uneasily, because in Acts II and III time is spent to narrate in an unconvincing way the interim actions. In Act II, the Emperor knows, and Cébès knows he knows, why Cébès is there, but Cébès has to tell him—tell, really, the audience—that "Tête d'or had me stored in your palace, Sire! I know I'm in the way. But he'll have to come back soon,/If he wants to see his goods alive!" (93). Another aesthetic weakness is that only Cébès, Simon Agnel, and the Princess really project their personalities. The author *was* the two first, *believed in* the last. Furthermore, only Cébès and Simon do justice to the poetic line used throughout the play, and even here the results are not consistently ideal. *Tête d'or* is more literary than theatrical.

The play presents a state of mind that is universal in an aesthetic and convincing way despite the weakness of the whole. As for *Tête d'or*'s "cosmic" worth, beyond what has been said, the play portrays a very selfish individual. The mental state and the glimmering of a probable solution in God are no more than that. The hero's travels in space and through society are metaphorical, in that he does not begin with or acquire a social sense. This is not to say that the play has philosophical limitations. More exactly, it has set for itself philosophical limits. In all, one senses that the author of *Tête d'or* is a budding aesthetic and moral genius. He is not quite himself yet in two senses: He is still borrowing and he is still developing. *René* and *Tête d'or* are in countless ways very different, but it would seem reasonable to assume that more lovers of literature would prefer the latter to the former.

It need hardly be pointed out how this play relates to its twenty-one-year-old composer. Biblical woman-figure, personal and Rimbaldian aspects of the poet-hero, dislike of the times, interior combat between return of belief and formal conversion, Villeneuve geography.

III   *LA VILLE, 1st v.*

La Ville, written in 1890, a year after *Tête d'or*, seems a step
backward aesthetically. The three-acter has thirty-odd named
dramatis personae plus innumerable "masons, workers, townsmen,
officers, children, men, women." The setting is Paris, whose
crowded animation in the time of the play's composition explains
the incessant coming-and-going onstage. The effect does not quite
come off. Isidore de Besme, the engineer, expresses and personifies the city's malady:

> ... There is nothing.
> Yes! There is nothing.
> There all of you are, very happy. But listen:
> I have seen and touched
> The horror of uselessness, not to speak of the proof of it in my own
> hands (I; VII, 34).

Some hope is offered in Thalie, who proposes marriage to
Coeuvre the poet. In Act II Avare (Miser), a civic leader, exhorts the populace to anarchy:

> It's all over.
> Peace will no longer be here among us, for a quarrel separates man
> from man, as dogs from wolves.
> You'll have to strangle me, or I'll devour your bowels!
> May misfortune be your lot,
> Bad luck to all you rich people! A curse on you! (75-76)

The third act shows a devastated city. Into the vacuum come
the forces of religion. The last half of the act catechizes on what
a religious monarchy should be. Religion—for in the first two-
and-a-half acts there is not a single sacral reference—and a prince,
one Ivors, are duly invested. The religion is no doubt Roman
Catholicism. The picture is what the author would have liked the
ancien régime to be, not what it really had been.

"Chronological accretion" makes it progressively more unrea-
sonable or difficult to examine a work by Claudel unto itself
alone; too many verbal gymnastics would be needed for perse-
verance in that approach. Suffice it to say that the message is
obvious: The City must eschew materialism, but anarchy is not
the means, only godliness is. If *Tête d'or* was selfish in a certain
sense, one can fully suspect that Claudel's own motives were far
from selfish. He probably blocked out his solutions. His first play

would show a personal one, an active life curbed by belief in the
hereafter. There was no great need to bring in religion by name,
since by semantic definition it is social. The second play would
by negative example show what godliness does to the City, then
by catechistic means show a city enlightened by God. Of this
duet the second play is a marked failure, for the very reasons
that inspired him to write it. His own confusion in the face of the
confusion of Paris resulted in the play's confusion. His presentation and solution of the problem are idealistic and none of the
countless characters is endowed with Claudel's own emotions, at
least not as are Simon Agnel and Cébès. At the onset it was said
that *La Ville* seems an aesthetic regression. This may misstate
the case, if *Tête d'or* and *La Ville* were conceived as has been
suggested. Rather, the right-hand side of the diptych—*La Ville*—
is of lesser quality than the left-hand side, for most understandable reasons. Much later, Claudel said of the two plays: "*La Ville*
was written, as distinguished from *Tête d'or*, right in the midst
of my efforts to convert."[6] This does not mean that in 1889 he was
not laboring toward formal conversion. Rather, one year later the
struggle simply became more intense and there were doubtless
last-minute flurried uprisings of the devil's advocate within him.
It is this pressure that voiced itself in the hyper-confusion of *La
Ville*'s first two-and-a-half acts, and in the unconvincingness of
the dénouement's serenity.

Good or bad, like any Claudelian play *La Ville* shows richly
both the author at the time of writing, and many of his themes.
Some character-names such as Thalie, Angèle, Laure, and Audivine ("Divine Water" phonetically, thus holy water or grace) tell
their own story. The name of the poet Coeuvre tells more than
one: first, the name contains the word for work or deed (oeuvre),
which reflects the semantic meaning of the word poet. Second,
Coeuvres is an Aisne place-name. Isidore de Besme, engineer, announces the architect theme. Avare is a Rimbaud-figure.

IV   *LA JEUNE FILLE VIOLAINE, 1st v.*

Tête d'or and *La Ville* point forward to Claudel's formal conversion. *La Jeune Fille Violaine*, composed in 1892 and 1893, looks
back on it. The action of the play's four parts is clear, or at least
clearer than that of the two plays that had preceded it. The place
is Combernon, the real name of a real farm, many of whose

buildings are medieval, within brief walking distance of Villeneuve. Violaine and Bibiane Vercors both love Jacquin Uri, their
father's foreman. Bibiane persuades Jacquin that Violaine and
Eloi Baube are lovers. Although promised to one Lidine, Baube
in effect does love Violaine, who chooses not to deny her sister's
allegations of unfaithfulness. The father Anne Vercors has decided to quit Combernon. He has owned it for forty years, been
married to Elisabeth for thirty, and the first seven years of their
union had been sterile. Now he will set out on a pilgrimage to the
sea, where he shall be spiritually cleansed, that is, "dematerial-
ized" in preparation for death. There is a time to live and a time
to die.

Unaware of Bibiane's schemings, he leaves family and Combernon under the belief that Violaine and Jacquin will wed. This
is not to be. Instead, Violaine voluntarily departs as well. As she
does, Bibiane throws cinders in her face. Bibiane and Jacquin
marry and have a son Aubin, born blind. Realizing that this is a
mystical punishment, one wintry night when Aubin is five,
Bibiane decides to visit, in the nearby forest of Le Géyn, the
thaumaturge called l'Aveugle, or the Blind One. She does not
know that this is actually Violaine, who had eventually become
blind because of the ashes cast into her eyes. Coincidentally, just
before her visit, Baube, now married to Lidine, has also been to
see Violaine. The latter persades him to accept his life as it is.
Violaine and Bibiane are mutually surprised by their encounter.
Bibiane tells her that their mother is dead, that their father has
not yet come back. At dawn, Aubin is cured of his blindness, with
Violaine's intercession but through Bibiane's own faith. The
mother returns with her son. Jacquin suspects the truth and still
recalls his love for Violaine. Jealous, desirous of solidarizing her
family, at the end of the following summer Bibiane lures her
sister to a place near Combernon, where she fatally wounds her.
Violaine is discovered and carried home to die. The truth is
learned. Among others, the now pregnant Lidine comes to Violaine's side. The saintly sister persuades the whole household to
forgive.

Just after her death, Anne Vercors returns; he had visited Rome
after having gone to the sea. Unperturbed by all he learns, he
successfully concludes Violaine's attempts at restoring general
harmony. Spiritually, he is now as little of this world as had been

66

 Violaine from the beginning. Toward the end, he "sings" of the peace that has come over his family, of the beloved Combernon, of the golden harvest-time—all these things being parts of God's creation.

From the play's viewpoint, Violaine's movements through time and space have effectively only had to do with saintly things. Her death in itself is merely a change in state. Relatively, it stabilizes two marriages. For her life of renunciation, sacrifice, suffering, purity, prayer, healing, love, and good counsel, she receives a personal reward she scarcely needs, becoming as it were the spiritual mother of Aubin and of Baube's child-to-be.

Except for its coherent series of actions, what is not included in a basic summary of plot and meaning in *La Jeune Fille Violaine* is what best reflects Claudel's growing concern with perfecting his dramatic techniques. First of all, he labored to make the reader-spectator sense Combernon as a living entity. Two apt illustrative scenes in Act I, more or less duplicating each other, show Anne, then Violaine, speaking to the farm children. Anne:

> When the ducks get off their roosts, when the poultry heads to the water,
> When the rooster takes the hens off for a piss.
> When I was young, little ones. . . .

> Lentil-beans were as broad as quoits, plums were as big as donkey-turds. Peaches
> Burst wide open, splattering their sugar on the leaves (VII, 243).

Violaine's tale is more decorous, full of animals and a moral, about "an old man who had never wanted to get married" (248). Elisabeth the mother is very convincing too. If her role as a good peasant wife, simplicity itself, is as easy to portray as the naturalistic servants that abound in literature, the point is elsewhere: She evidences Claudel's growing desire for local color, that is, for convincing stage happenings. Also, his desire for characterization. Violaine the fair and Bibiane the dark "live," as do Anne, Elisabeth, Jacquin. *Tête d'or* succeeds where *La Ville* fails because Claudel pictured himself in Cébès and Simon Agnel, believed in the Princess. But that was no lasting general solution. A playwright cannot project himself into or sympathize utterly with all his characters. Most of them must have lives of their own. At

least, these are truths in Claudel's context. An important feature
of the first Violaine play is that Claudel identifies with his characters, and not vice versa.

Yet Claudel disowned this first version more than he did his
other first versions. God vies for Violaine, so do two men; there
are too many rivals. Also, there is her double spiritual maternity,
and the similar scenes Anne and Violaine have with the children.
When Baube visits the refuge, if he can give Violaine some news
of her family, how can he not know that she had not married
Jacquin? Why does Anne return just when Violaine is murder-
ously assaulted? Claudel, one could say, was beginning to curb
himself, but only beginning.

The serenity shared by Violaine and Anne is not so much
Claudel's in 1893, although he was at least serene in his beliefs
and practices. Rather, it is a serenity he aspired to and was
tempted by. An agent in this was his reading in mystics and
saints. In general, it was time for a peaceful play like *La Jeune
Fille Violaine:* Something was needed to celebrate Christmas Day
1890. At this time Claudel was also reading the Greek and Latin
classics, more in translation than in the original, but sometimes
in both concurrently. As a result of this and of his special interest in Aeschylus, he translated and/or rendered into literary
French the first part of the *Oresteia. Agamemnon* was composed
more or less sporadically from 1892 through 1894, over much the
same time he was writing the Violaine play. Both were completed in America. Some of the latter's relative clarity is no doubt
ascribable to Claudel's interest at that time in the classics.

V   *L'ECHANGE, 1st v.*

Claudel spent almost all 1893 and 1894 in America, first in
New York, then in Boston. His immediate theatrical reaction was
L'Echange, a product of those same years. The setting is the
country where it was written, so very different from his own. The
plot is relatively classical: The three unities and the *convenances*
(proprieties) are adhered to; there are only four roles; the action
is simple. The time is 1890, the place the beach of an estate on
the East Coast (Maine?). Thomas Pollock Nageoire is the pro-
prietor; Lechy Elbernon, an actress, is his mistress; Louis Laine,
half-Indian and twenty years old, is his groundskeeper; and

Marthe—twenty-three—is Louis' French wife. Only six months ago he had met and married her in France. Marthe is unhappy in the new land; Louis is unhappy at the restraints imposed by marriage and by a full-time job. Pollock is attracted to Marthe and offers to buy her from Louis, who would just as soon cut his traces anyway. Marthe, the epitome of traditional France, will have nothing of this. But money has been tendered and accepted. Under Lechy's orders a colored hired hand kills Louis as he rides off. She meanwhile sets fire to Pollock's bungalow, wherein his entire fortune is contained.

A moral is hard to find in this first *Echange,* beyond the fact that the action itself implies a judgment against America. More universally, an illicit exchange took place and one of the guilty parties was punished by death. Marthe was good from the beginning. It is not very sure that Pollock or Lechy have profited from the events. The play contains many ideas and symbols. Lechy speaks of the actress' profession; Marthe and Pollock both look on financial transactions as sacrosanct. Marthe also personifies traditional values. In addition, she represents all womankind. Both Louis and Pollock commonly address her as either "Bittersweet" or its French equivalent "Douce-Amère," and many times one or the other proceeds to explain that woman is sweet as an inspirer and as a helpmate of man, bitter in her commonsensical role as man's second conscience. All in all, her sacrificial nature makes her more sweet than bitter. As for Louis, he depicts the footlooseness and irresponsibility latent in human nature. His being a "vanishing American" adds to this depiction and, incidentally, Claudel paid almost naturalistic attention to the Indian details of the play.[7]

Externally, one knows that Claudel meant the four characters to mirror various aspects of himself.[8] His penchant toward total liberty, especially moral, is shown through the "loose" actress Lechy; his loathing of responsibility, that is, desire for another sort of liberty, is reflected in Louis; Marthe of course has the values he had admired in France and which he himself had or would have liked to have had. Despite himself, he was becoming adept as a counsular representative of France; in this way, Pollock stands for him. At the same time, there is a distinction between these four characters and the hero and anti-hero of *Tête d'or.* These last two incorporate viscerally their author. The first four symbolize him. That Claudel was also translating Aeschylus at the time reinforces the suggestion that Louis is punished for braving the gods.

Unless a masterpiece must be perfect in all respects, *L'Echange* is his first dual one—both dramatic and poetic. His poetry was no doubt aided by the characters' affinities to himself, but since this is a limited relationship, the only conclusion is that Claudel's abilities at artistic personification remained at least on a par with those he had demonstrated in the first *Jeune Fille Violaine*. More likely, they had improved. Dramatically, *L'Echange* is a masterpiece by virtue of the successful simplification of his gifts. The progress was basically commonsensical, though partly explicable perhaps by his involvement with Aeschylus and by his reaction against the plot weaknesses of the first Violaine play.

L'Echange is not perfect. The "holy" view of business is expressed most inappropriately, through the rapacious and amoral Pollock; women cast as actresses exist onstage; they do not extemporize at length on their art. It is better for actresses to incarnate womanly virtues than for male actors to declaim them; the three other characters are kept busy telling Marthe all about what a woman's woman she is. These are sore points one senses Claudel did not feel as such. A minor shortcoming stems from Claudel's growing concern for local color: the play is larded with terms or words supposed to be American but which are sometimes neither that, nor British English: "Take that, man I say!" (I; VIII, 32); "I like some drink" (III;82).

VI   TETE D'OR, 2nd v.

Toward the end of his stay in America, and five years after the first version, Claudel found time to write another *Tête d'or*, his first "second version". Now unshakeable in his faith, Claudel was in what could be called his first period of serenity. In *La Jeune Fille Violaine* one easily perceives this. The first *Tête d'or* parallels and benefits from Claudel's personal tensions. That those tensions had eased by 1894 is amply illustrated in the second. Simon Agnel is no longer as ferocious. When he becomes a believer, he is much more the proselytizer to his men; thus there is a serious break with one of the very foundation stones of the 1889 version, namely, the mirrorings of his own tensions at that

time. To compensate for this "watering down," Claudel had re-
course to Simon Agnel's didacticism, and also to a certain "poetic"
intensification. For instance, the tree that in 1889 was already a
sign of the earth-to-heaven metaphor is much more stressed in
1894.

Perhaps the second *Tête d'or* testifies to Claudel's realization
that he could not forever depend on his own self as such a complete source for the personalities of any of his characters. Whether this be the case, or whether the change in the 1894 play and
in its title character is due to Claudel's own evolution, the fact
remains that the greatest value of the 1889 version—the depiction
of youth's revolutionary *état d'âme*—is somewhat sapped in its
subsequent form. These subtleties are naturally more apparent to
the reader than to the theatergoer. They are not so plain even
to the former, who has to look for them between two texts that
are lexically very often the same. It is not appropriate to look to
the second *Tête d'or* for improvements or steps backward in
Claudel's art. He was too close to the old text and to his new life
—one a mental attachment, the other a visceral one—to make of
the second *Tête d'or* a work as independent as subsequent second
versions would prove to be.[9]

VII *LE REPOS DU SEPTIEME JOUR*

It was of course in China that Claudel wrote *Le Repos du
septième jour* (1895-1896; *And on the seventh day God rested*).
Easily his least dramatic play, *Le Repos* has essentially only one
character, the Emperor of an Eastern kingdom that must be an
artistic transposition of China. His subjects are unhappy. In
search of the explanation of this, the Emperor descends into the
Underworld, where he becomes blind. Self-defeatingly, the
demonic anti-gods provide it: Man has forgotten or chosen to
ignore that this world is held in trust for God by men. The re-
minder of this truth is the seventh day, when, laying aside his
material possessions and resting from his labors, man devotes
himself to praise of God. Leprous now as well as blind, the
Emperor returns to his land with a cross, passes on his Kingdom
to his son, and withdraws to a mountain to found the first
monastery.

A great problem for many Christians, obviously shared by the
author, is how to explain revelation and God's love before the fact

of non-Christian cultures. *Le Repos* says that God and many
other aspects of the Hebraic-Christian religions are in universal
evidence but are simply overlooked in some parts of creation.
God sends his signs, such as the cross, which is coincidentally
the Sino-Japanese hieroglyphic for the number 10. *Le Repos* is
not clear on the final enlightenment, that is, the agent that would
make a China-like country change from a Christian-like cult
(what the Emperor plans to establish on his mountain) to a truly
Christian one. It could be through the combination of missionaries and divine signs. Or, in the same way that the Old Testament is held to announce the First Coming, perhaps the signs
(the spiritual values of the East, belief in a hell, sometimes in
a single deity, the symbol for ten) prophesy the Second.

Innumerable sources for *Le Repos* spring to mind. Virgil,
Dante, Orpheus, Christ: all are associated with a visit to the
Underworld. Many Eastern religions have a hell; ancient Japanese scrolls could well illustrate Dante's *Inferno.* Claudel had to
express: his views on why, all the same, the East was not Christian; his apocalyptic hope for the East's religious future. The
missionaries he knew in China must have talked in veins like
these. He was a proselytizer himself and also was tempted to
retire to a monastery. *Le Repos* was one means (as *Connaissance
d l'Est* was another) to express the East he knew, and furthermore the relief he felt there after his two years in America.

The catechistic end of the first *Ville* and the sections of the
first *Violaine* where Ann Vercors "forgets" he is in a play and re-
cites a poem about harvest time and the whole universe: one sees
in these scenes instances of Claudel's extra-theatrical preoccupations taking over his pen in the midst of writing a drama. *Le
Repos* reverses this tendency. It is dominated by nontheatrical
concerns that are invaded only slightly by dramatic considerations. It is thus the second consecutive play by Claudel that
shows little or no promise of his development as a dramatic poet.
The second *Tête d'or* tried an impossible task and the results
were inadequate, as expected. Neither, though, does *Le Repos*
mark arrested progress or regressions: Claudel's aims were simply
elsewhere than in improving his dramatic artistry.

VIII   *LA VILLE,* 2nd v.

The second *Ville* was finished in 1897, while he was still in

China. The new cast numbers a more sensible eight. The city is no longer Paris; it is simply *la ville*. The mayor is Lambert de Besme, weak-willed and aging. His brother Isidore is the city's "engineer." Avare, of mysterious origins, can incite the populace to action through his spoken word. Coeuvre the poet has an almost official status as such. Lambert is a Pygmalion-like figure in that he wants to marry his ward, Lâla. The "lesson" of the second *Ville* is similar, though told more simply. Coeuvre, not Lambert, eventually marries Lâla. After bearing his son Ivors she leaves him to live with Avare.

Galatea turned Cassandra, she is given to speaking oracularly, notably on woman's role: "Woman is closer to the earth than you men" (II; VII, 187); "I am the promise which cannot be kept" (III; 229). Lambert fades away and dies; Avare brings on his all-leveling revolution, but he is not quite so anarchic. He reigns with more than a semblance of order over the razed city, but can come up with no further solution. He leaves, despite the pleas of his two lieutenants, Thyrsée and Gérin. The catechistic formula of the end is different, but the import is about the same. Coeuvre reappears after an absence to be bishop of the City, and his son Ivors, who had been another of Avare's aides, is the City's Prince: "For ourself, settling down in the heart of the City, we shall constitute the laws" (230).

Since the first *Ville* was the idealistic half of the diptych, the version of seven years later did not have so much weighted against it as had the second *Tête d'or*. The element lost—its value is arguable—is the confused lyricism of the first, mirroring the author's 1890 *état d'âme*. Much is gained by Claudel's evolution from tension to serenity; most importantly the play also evolves from one to the other. Peace was gathering about Claudel in 1897—ever-strengthening faith, attraction to the contemplative life, the tranquillity of the Orient. Aeschylus is behind the second *Ville* for its simplification, for the person of Lâla. Most important for Claudel personally was that he himself was behind Coeuvre the poet-priest. To an extent, the Besme brothers, one weak, one strong, repeat the Cébès-Simon Agnel conflict within his own mind.

However one may judge Claudel's incurable predilection for having his characters stop the clock to declaim on professions and spiritual roles of one individual or a group of them, this is an extremely interesting and informative part of his whole production, particularly his theater. Here is the very end of a three-page long exchange on poetry between the Besme brothers (appearing in only the second *Ville*):

COEUVRE.—Oh Besme, I don't speak as a result of my desires; rather, I conceive in my sleep.

And I can't explain where I draw that breath, for the breath is drawn from me.

Swelling the emptiness within me, I open my mouth,

And, having inhaled air, in this his own legacy through which man at each second *exhales* the image of his own death.

I give back an intelligible word.

And, having said it, I know what I've said.

Thus I succeed bit by bit in making manifest your suffering (I; 154-155).

Shades of *L'Echange*, Mallarmé's *mardis*, Corneille! There are many similar passages in the second *Ville*, on poetry or on Woman. The world would be sorely deprived if such Baroque or Cornelian elements were absent. If some are bad aesthetically, they are all interesting, and certainly the independent gems more than pay for those parts of the catechism (Coeuvre: "What is the advantage of marriage, Lâla?"; I; 165) one does not care for. The preceding long quotation, incidentally, succinctly explains the process behind the Claudelian *verset* although there is the danger, against which one has already been warned, of seeing the psycho-physical breath as something purely physical. Historically the passage is coeval with much of *Connaissance de l'Est* (1895-1905—mostly 1900 or before), and surely Claudel's important *Art poétique* (1900-1904) was already being worked out, consciously and unconsciously.

Also, a concordance of Claudel's theater would probably show that the 1897 *Ville* marks a sudden, vast upsurge in his use of simile words like *comme* and *ainsi*. The universal analogy was nothing new to him in 1897, but the year is crucial to his application of the concept with the extra stipulation of "under God." Crucial not because of any dramatic event in his life just then, but because his techniques had evolved to that point at that time.

IX   LA JEUNE FILLE VIOLAINE, 2nd v.

The second *Jeune Fille Violaine* (1898-1900) was begun in

74 PAUL CLAUDEL

China and completed in France. The most important dramatic
change is that one Pierre de Craon (this last word is pronounced
in two syllables) generally replaces the Lidine-Baube pair. In the
first act a civil engineer, a bridge-builder, Pierre later becomes
an architect. He and Violaine open the play. Pierre had stopped
overnight at Combernon and now is about to be off, before dawn.
Paradoxically, he uplifts Violaine by dint of his own spiritual
strength, though he had already felt physical passion for her. The
moment is special in two ways. It marks Pierre's absolute separation from earthly cares. From now on, he will live as would a
priest. He realizes also that Violaine is at a fork in the road.
Either she can marry, or she can follow Pierre's way. He exhorts
her to make the higher choice. Departing, he kisses her, motivated
by his now pure love. Mara—Hebrew for "bitter"; she is the first
version's Bibiane—witnesses the kiss and chooses to interpret it
to her own ends. Jacquin Uri is now Jacques Hury. Violaine as
before allows his jealousy to go uncorrected. She leaves, under
more or less the same conditions. Anne does too, but this time for
America, where his dead brother's children need looking after.
At the dénouement both Anne and Pierre coincidentally return.

From the first *Violaine* have been eliminated many local color
elements; the result is a loftier play. No longer do Anne and Violaine speak to the farm children in a way suggesting total recall
on the part of the author. The earthy peasants Lidine and Baube
are replaced by a single individual, the priestly Pierre de Craon.
Offsetting this evolution slightly is the fact that now Anne goes
to America, instead of to the sea and Rome:

ANNE VERCORS.—The soil is good; they don't know how to cultivate.
I don't like the people there.
PIERRE DE CRAON.—Neither do I.
ANNE VERCORS.—Good? Can you say soil is good when it gives up its
products without real work? With their machines!
It's all soft. . . .
They don't like work. Their fruit is watery; they harvest a suspect
richness.
And since they don't know how to work, they don't know how to
enjoy what they earn. Nothing turns as ripe as it should.
Like decrepit old men, they like sweet things; they eat candy and
drink lemonade.
Everything's made mechanically, the body's clothes and the mind's
(IV; VII, 414).

Of course, Pierre de Craon intensifies Claudel's personal drama of the period, as already depicted in the second *Ville's* Ivors and in *Le Repos'* Emperor. Claudel, too, was beginning to "separate" himself, or hoping he would be allowed to. Pierre, who has been seduced by the water of grace ("L'eau m'a séduit"; I; 334—think of the first *Ville's* Audivine), is a builder of bridges and aqueducts. No doubt a play is intended on the semantic origin of the word metaphor. Simon Agnel as well as Coeuvre could talk like a poet; and now Pierre begins a long speech with "The word, young maiden,/Isn't formed like a note under the organist's finger when his foot pushes on the pedal" (1; 330).

All men are poets in the broadest sense. Although nominally four acts long, the second *Violaine* has in effect five acts, or four acts and the prologue, that is, the long opening scene of Act I between Pierre and Violaine; in fact, the next version of the play, the 1910-1911 *Annonce faite à Marie*, does have a prologue, so called, and four acts.

Simpler, the 1898-1900 version is for that a better play than the first. It is also more serenely beautiful. One must look, though, with nostalgia upon the stronger local color and characterization of the first. Exclusive of considerations about aesthetic unity, one might well in fact prefer the other sort of authenticity to be found in the *Violaine* of 1892 and 1893.

X *Evolution of the Dramatist Through 1900*

The second version is the last play of an unofficial cycle. Claudel was never to lose a taste for divigations. His characters would never cease to lay aside their masks and declaim on such varied subjects as womankind, poetizing, separation, America, and acting. Yet some such instances do not overly intrude on the action. If in *L'Echange* the eulogies on business and businessmen are not apropos in the context of the amoral Pollock, the side-poems of the second *Violaine* are often most beautiful, and always apt enough. *L'Echange* is a masterpiece with flaws. The second *Violaine* is unflawed, well constructed, a good compromise between poetry and drama, with the poetic line always matching the personage and the occcasion.

The most interesting thread in the development from the 1889 *Tête d'or* to the 1900 *Jeune Fille Violaine* is Claudel's growing prowess as a dramatic poet and as a dramatist. The *verset* gets better and more appropriate, the action simplifies and clarifies. From 1900 through 1924 and the completion of *Le Soulier de satin*, Claudel wrote his main plays with a constant appropriateness of line vis-à-vis of character and situation. Therefore, until this study reaches the third period of Claudelian drama it will generally refrain from commenting much in this area.

Another intriguing thread is the evolution from tension to serenity in Claudel's own makeup from 1886 to 1900, and the effect each stage of the evolution exerted both on choice of subject matter and on successful treatment of subject. Tense in 1889, he chose to show himself through a much-suffering hero, Tête d'or. This aspect of the play comes off well. One year later, though perhaps he had conceived of it in 1889, *La Ville* proved too theoretical for his taut *état d'âme*. The physical tension of Paris itself went against the ability to adequately transpose that tension. The first *Jeune Fille Violaine, composed in* 1892-1893 by a firm and serene convert, derives from these conditions its tranquil subject and relatively successful treatment. *L'Echange* has *per se* a subject neither tense nor serene. The second *Tête d'or* is weakened because its *raison d'être* and strongest asset are tensions no longer felt by the man who wrote it. *Le Repos du septième jour* is out of the question. The second *Ville* gains for the same reasons the second *Tête d'or* loses. In 1897 Claudel was in a state to provide from his marrow the calm solution proposed by *La Ville*. Last of all, either of the first two *Violaine*'s is a mystical play. From the point of view of unity, the regretted local color and characterization are then malapropos. The play's calm subject benefits from Claudel's firmness of faith in 1900. Yet there is an obstruction. He was not satisfied with himself then, was probably never wholly satisfied with himself. At any rate, the desire to be purer, to be a priest or a monk, was either a new tension or an extension of one that could be termed perpetual Christian dissatisfaction with the self. Believably, both Pierre de Craon and Violaine separate themselves from a regular worldly existence and, at the same time, yearn for what they give up. Of course, the tension-security struggle is so important to Claudel's theater because it, and his whole work, are always a mirror-image of him just when he had pen in hand.

A third thread resembles the second. From 1886 to 1900 Claudel evolved from a certain tension to a certain security. But there were to be two other tensions, and their resolutions, corresponding with his two subsequent dramatic periods. All the same, throughout his life Claudel evolved toward absolute serenity, and in his theater this is shown by a lifelong or secular evolution in techniques and interests, from earth toward heaven, as opposed to the ups and downs in periods of his life, but which also took the same direction upward, from the visible to the invisible. A discussion of these two tensions is better placed later on, but they concern his great sin of the early 1900's and his semi-abandonment of secular literature in the late 1920's. Of historical interest is the 1901 publication of some of Claudel's first plays under the significant title of *L'Arbre* (*The tree*). The collection included *L'Echange, Le Repos du septième jour,* the second versions of *Tête d'or, La Ville, La Jeune Fille Violaine.*

B. SECOND PERIOD 1905-1924

Partage de midi (1905); *L'Otage* (1908-1910); *L'Annonce faite à Marie* (1910-1911); *Protée* (1913); *Le Pain dur* (1913-1914); *Les Choéphores* (1913-1915); *La Nuit de Noël 1914* (1915); *Les Euménides* (1913-1916); *Le Père humilié* (1915-1916); *L'Ours et la lune* (1917); *L'Homme et son désir* (1917); *La Femme et son ombre* (1922); *Le Soulier de satin* (1919-1924); *La Parabole du festin* (1924).

Six of these plays are of prime importance: *Partage de midi,* the *Otage* trilogy (*L'Otage, Le Pain dur, Le Père humilié*), *L'Annonce faite à Marie, Le Soulier de satin.*

I PARTAGE DE MIDI, 1st v.

Partage de midi tells of Ysé and Mesa, who meet on a boat bound for the Orient. Mesa is a customs official; Ysé is the wife of an engineer, De Ciz; he and their several children are also on board; so is Amalric, Mesa's good friend. Both Amalric and De Ciz are soldiers of fortune, but where the former is strong and well off, the latter is weak and of modest means. Amalric knew Ysé before she married. All four central characters are in their thirties. Mesa is a bachelor. His vocation for the priesthood has just been found wanting, and his glumness pervades attempts at shipboard cheer. The action begins on a hot day at noon. Suez is behind, the glistening sea all round.

MESA.—Noon in the sky. Noon in the middle of our life.

And here we are together, round the same age of our moment, in the center of the complete horizon, free, unpacked.

Unstuck from the earth, looking backward and forward.

YSE.—Behind us water and before us still more water.

DE CIZ.—How bitter it is to have stopped being young!....

MESA.—How fearful to have stopped being alive!

AMALRIC.—How great it is not to be dead, but to be living (I; XI, 20).

Later, awkwardly, Mesa approaches Ysé, who in her deckchair is reading a love story: One thinks of Paolo and Francesca. They talk of love. They both sense that they are in love, that their love is star-crossed, but talk round the truth. Finally:

YSE.—Mesa, I'm Ysé, it's I.

MESA.—It's too late.

It's all over. Why are you looking for me?

YSE.—Haven't I found you?

MESA.—It's all over! I wasn't waiting for you.

I had it all set up so well.

I was going to go away, to remove myself from the company of men, it was all arranged!

Why are you looking for me? why are you bothering me?

YSE.—That's what women are made for (I; 34).

They speak on. Their whole duet is one of the most beautiful passages in all of Claudel's literature. Later on in Hong Kong, Mesa monologs on his destiny. The carnal liaison he is on the point of entering into is as far a cry as possible from his recently refused vocation. Revenge against his God? Guilt invades him. Ultimately, like David getting rid of Uriah the Hittite, he sends De Ciz away on a perilous mission. Ysé has second thoughts, tries to dissuade her husband, but by now he is caught up with the prospects like a child and leaves. Ysé feels the full impact of the sin too. A few months later, when she is pregnant with Mesa's child, she leaves him to live with Amalric. Ysé hopes the latter is just enough stronger than herself to allow the two of them to live compatibly. She bears the child. Meanwhile revolution is brewing. There seems no way to escape the revolutionaries. Rather than letting his "family" fall into their hands, Amalric sets a charge under the house. But Mesa appears, with a pass. He is attacked by Amalric and left to die. The latter and Ysé depart to board a ship that will take them to freedom, though before she leaves she kills her child, wanting no link with the past. Alone, Mesa revives. It is night time; the sky is clear:

My mortuary chapel!
Everywhere, to the right and left, the forest of torches surrounding me!
Not lighted candles, but powerful stars, like great flaming maidens
Before God's face, such as, in holy paintings, one sees Mary feeling her unworthiness!
And myself, the man, the Intelligent One,
Here I lie on the Earth, ready to die, as on a solemn catafalque (III; 91-92).

The whole of "Le Cantique de Mesa"—so referred to in the text—is another highspot in Claudel's literature, recapturing the playwright's tortured *état d'âme* as he resolves intellectually what his weak flesh cannot accept. Ysé returns, and they make their peace. Their love was wrong, but it was right. They prepared to die, not in desperation but victoriously. Mesa:

. . . all veils lowered, myself, the strong fulminating flame, the great male in God's glory,
Man in the splendor of August, the conquering Spirit in the transfiguration at Noon! (III; 106)

In the normal sense, *Partage de midi* is the least poetic of Claudel's long plays. It is too close to truth to be concerned with prosody. Yet because prosody's aim is ultimate truth, and in the light of Claudel's understanding of the word poem, *Partage* is his most poetic play. Enough has been said in the preceding chapters about the truth behind the play and the importance of this play as regards that sort of truth. Many of the regular themes are present, as the plot summary and the quotations indicate. *Partage* is nourished by a new tension that is completely in spirit with it. Obviously, the Beatrice theme is not new in it. The theme has already been exemplified in the Princess of *Tête d'or*, in Lâla of the second *Ville*. Violaine of course uplifts the men in her life(though in the second *Jeune Fille Violaine* Pierre does this more for her than she for him). Before *Partage*, Claudel was concerned with the paradox of sin's existence in a universe created by love; he saw it as serving a mysterious purpose. The play and the experience behind it blended the ideas of earthly love and sin's necessity. *Etiam peccata*—sins also serve—refers to all sin; the phrase in a Claudelian context means especially carnal love, which excludes love toward God. Claudel no doubt held these positions before *Partage*, but beginning with it they gained a visceral quality laced with more certainty, and with guilt. Aesthetics aside, the play can well provide an excruciating vicarious experience for the reader-spectator.

II   *L'OTAGE and the Trilogy*

Claudel started *L'Otage* (*The hostage*) in 1908 in China and completed it two years later in Prague. It was to be the first play of a trilogy. This is evidenced in a May 1, 1908, letter to Gabriel Frizeau, written by Claudel after his return to France:

I'm tired now of fragmentary works, and I'd like to lock myself up for several years in something of whole cloth. Since I can't write an epic poem, I'd like to compose a cycle of dramas not producing just people, but the *ensemble* of strange, multiple and convergent means whereby these very people are produced for ends foreseen by God. (I believe I wrote you a word about this idea three years ago.) It's fairly possible that I take as a framework an audaciously re-arranged nineteenth-century story, in which I distinguish three interesting phenomena: 1st the French Revolution, which I'll call *the revolution against chance;* 2nd *knowledge of the earth;* 3rd *separation of earth and man* who no longer has any attachments to it (according to ascetic recommendations!!).[10]

The main characters are the cousins Georges and Sygne de Coûfontaine, Toussaint Turelure, the priest Badilon, Pope Pius VII (the hostage of the title). The opening scene occurs in 1812, in the Abbey of the Coûfontaine Cistercians, which Sygne has purchased.

Alone, Sygne has repaired the family estate after the revolutionary ravages, an opening symbol of which is the large crucifix on the wall, whose bronze Christ has been patched together. For twenty years Georges has been an émigré in Great Britain. Now he returns. His wife had been mistress of the Dauphin, but she and the two children died of fever. Sygne describes to Georges the job of rehabilitation she had to undertake:

The long hours of battle in notaries' offices, where you fight fully disguised and with a laughing face,

As once did my ancestors, with their visors lowered and their shields tight against their chests,
Myself a pitiful girl among the men of law like Joan of Arc among the warriors!
Visits to the prefect, discussions with farmers and middlemen ...
(I, 1; X, 23).

Georges and Sygne, attached to the past, swear an engagement oath, to continue the bloodline. He is an atheist; Sygne's faith is strong.

It eventually comes out in this, their first conversation since his return, that Georges has rescued the pope from imprisonment during Napoleon's absence from France and actually has brought him to Coûfontaine. They decide to hide him there. Baron Turelure loves Sygne. His mother had been her wetnurse, his father a sorcerer. The baron himself had played a full share in the massacre and pillaging at the Abbey and dependent monastery; before this, he had himself been a novice for awhile. Now, riding the Revolutionary crest, he is Prefect of the Marne. He comes to Coûfontaine, tells Sygne he knows the pope is there, and lets her choose between marrying him or having the pope reimprisoned. Because of her mutual oath with Georges and because Turelure is so repugnant to her, she refuses. Then her confessor Badilon persuades her to take the other choice. She does. In the passage of two years, Napoleon's fortunes are again on the wane. Sygne has had a child by Turelure, now Prefect of the Seine. He defends Paris against Louis XVIII, but only perfunctorily and self-seekingly. Georges must deed his lands to Sygne's child and the king must accept to be a constitutional monarch. This is all agreed to. Georges afterward tries to shoot Turelure but the latter fires at him and kills him. Sygne, protecting her husband, is mortally wounded by her cousin's shot. Before she dies, she is asked to accept her situation as Turelure's spouse and as a member of the new régime. She makes a gesture with her hand, which almost surely indicates no.

Although Claudel feared that *L'Otage* would harm him professionally because it would be interpreted as anti-republican, the play is not altogether pro-*ancien régime*. Before 1789 France was sick politically. Afterward too it was sick. He saw this, and his political position, in life and in art, was always to make do with what was. This despite his yearning for a properly functioning

religious monarchy, as prescribed at the end of either *Ville*. But
of course in this latest play it is again a question of a dream transposed, not of a prophesy recorded. It need not be repeated that
in the play itself Georges' wife was the Dauphin's mistress,
Georges himself an atheist.

L'Otage lacks the personal point of view expressed in all that
had preceded. His letter to Frizeau indicates that Claudel conceived of *L'Otage* as the first of three related studies to show that
the loss of hierarchic inter-relationships had been the cost of the
French Revolution. At the same time, looking into that period,
the end of the eighteenth century, he saw that it was not then
that the decay had started. This explains why, after the first play
of the trilogy, he did not immediately write the other two. There
will be more on this subject, apropos of his next play, the medieval *Annonce faite à Marie*.

L'Otage is still not ultra-realistic. Pius VII (1800-1823) expe-
rienced nothing like what the fictional pope experiences. Symbolic of the truth, it still adheres more closely to time-place considerations than anything that had gone before, and can be called
Claudel's first historical play. Since it is a question of 1812 to
1814 and an interpretation of the results of monarchy's downfall,
it certainly could not have viscerally concerned the 1908-1910
Claudel who wrote it. Thus it is more a play of ideas. But it was
a time in Claudel's life, when he felt a post-*Partage* tranquility,
that was ripe for such a play. And since Claudel was now an
accomplished dramatic poet, and dramatist, *L'Otage*, a relatively
impersonal work, is still one of his masterpieces. Claudel admitted
that Balzac's *Une Ténébreuse Affaire* influenced his play; the
plots indeed have much in common.[11]

III   *Violence and Sin in Claudel's Plays*

Simon Agnel is an assassin: Lâla and Lechy Elbernon flit between two mates; Mara (Bibiane) blinds Violaine, then slays her.
Ysé strangles her child. Sygne almost sells her soul, a most griev-
ous offense as compared to the death of even a pope. In fact,
Claudel wavered occasionally on such counts as these, to the
point, in a 1914 variant of the scene where Sygne refuses to accept her fate, of having her accept it in a Christian way. French
prelates have been known to complain energetically about the sin
in Claudel's theater.

Claudel was not suggesting these actions; he was telling what some invented people do. The actions are symbols of actions. Simon Agnel's crime is a mirror of something, not a murder, in Claudel's own life. Mara's can be construed as a sign of less sinful actions motivated by familial reasons. There is no real saint or martyr Violaine. Thus, it can be viewed as quite abstractly true that the physical death of one who had been so close to God when she was alive is inconsequential as compared to the necessity of a proper earthly union between Mara and Jacques (in the first *Violaine,* between Baube and Lidine, Bibiane and Jacquin). Badilon advises Sygne to wed Turelure and save the pope. The point is that this is what he advises and what she does. Neither are these theologically sound actions or reactions, nor did Claudel mean to defend them.

Involved here is a mixture of human nature studies and artistic transpositions. Sygne's choice is full of existentialist doubt, which incidentally evokes Jean-Paul Sartre, whose fiction and philosophy are sometimes considered as step-by-step guideposts to living, rather than general indications. Poor Sartre, poor Claudel, doubly so for being mentioned in the same breath. Sartre, urinator on Chateaubriand's memorial, conductor of invisible orchestras in dark closets, is no more the teeth-grinding campus purveyor of existentialism than was Claudel a seraph.

IV *L'ANNONCE FAITE A MARIE*

Mostly in Prague, in 1910 and 1911, he wrote his third Violaine play, calling it now *L'Annonce faite à Marie.* The second and third versions are complete rewritings as is the second *Ville* and as is not the second *Tête d'or. L'Annonce* takes place in the middle ages. Taking the cue from the quasi-temporal precision of *L'Otage* and despite the stage direction that the atmosphere is to be conventionally medieval, the action fits neatly into the third decade of the fifteenth century. A sacral ambience is studiously maintained throughout. Pierre de Craon is a master architect and builder of churches. He and Violaine have their encounter in a prologue so designated. A year before he had tried to rape her. She escaped with a knife wound on the arm. The very next day he had contracted leprosy. He is off to Rheims, whose craft guilds have commissioned him to build a church called Saint Justice, in

thanks to God for their town's prosperity. For the rest of France
and Christendom is in travail. There are two, on occasion three,
claimants to the papacy. France is further split by the English
occupation and by the weakness of the fleeting King, Charles VII.

Contrarily to the second *Violaine,* it is now the heroine who
uplifts the departing Pierre. She does say: "I'm Violaine, I'm
eighteen, my father's Anne Vercors, my mother's Elisabeth,/My
sister's called Mara, my fiancé Jacques. There, it's all set, there's
nothing else to know" (prologue; 20). But Pierre has already
asked: "Who are you, young maiden, and what then is that part
in you God has reserved for Himself . . . ?" (11). And she con-
tributes her engagement ring to his church. The leprosy had
killed all Pierre's chances for union with Violaine or with anyone
else. She still has to quell his lingering passion, and, for a higher
love, kisses him goodbye (not he her) with tears welling in her
eyes. Her fate or calling is cemented. Pierre has already said:
"The stone doesn't choose its place, rather, the Master Artisan
has chosen where it goes in the setting" (19). Mara's surprising
the kiss is superfluous as a reason for Violaine's departure, and
so is the fact of the leprosy-inducing kiss. Mara simply lets her
go. No cinders are needed. Mara knows somehow—mysteriously,
everyone except Jacques senses the play's secrets—that her sister,
purportedly bound to visit Jacques' mother before the wedding,
will really go to a leper refuge at Le Géyn. Act II, scene 3, when
Violaine fails to correct her finacé's doubts and even reinforces
them by showing him the flower of leprosy beneath her breast,
is one of the most moving scenes in all literature. One knows at
first more than Jacques: that the kiss was pure. The news of the
malady comes as a general surprise. Further revelations arrived
at on reflection are that from the moment of her catching leprosy,
she could not marry Jacques and, going back still further, that the
die was cast in the prologue: the tears, the voluntary assumption
of suffering, the gift of the engagement ring, the many indirect
references to the course in life that Violaine has already charted
for herself. The real drama of the scene stems therefore from
Violaine's reluctance *to accept with absolute willingness* what
it is now ordained that she must accept.

Anne Vercors leaves in this version for the reasons of the first—
self-purification in preparation for the hereafter—but also to
ameliorate, by a pilgrimage to the Holy Land, the travails of his

country and of all Christendom. He and Violaine say several times that they are too happy with normal destinies. The vocation of each thus takes them out of regular happiness and plants them in that of a higher variety. Mara comes to Violaine eight years later, on Christmas Eve, with the dead infant girl Aubaine, who had been her only child (no longer the blind boy-child Aubain). Violaine is not an established healer, just a blind lazar in a refuge, but Mara senses her saintliness and her potentialities as an intercessor. The child is resuscitated at dawn while Violaine holds it in her shawl. The eyes are now blue like Violaine's while before they had been black like Mara's and, also miraculously, there are beads of milk on the child's lips. Before the miracle, Charles VII and Joan of Arc pass nearby in the cortège bound for his coronation at Rheims. Though rendered much more poetic, the action of Act IV is about like that of the preceding version, except for noticeably more stress on the *etiam peccata* theme. There is one pope and one French king at the end. Anne's and Violaine's charitable actions and those of many others, for example, the prayers of the Queen Mother of France and the other cloistered nuns in the nearby convent of Monsanvierge (Mont Sainte Vierge, or Marymount), have exerted a beneficial effect on secular life.

Apropos of the train of thought that led from *L'Otage* to *L'Annonce*, Claudel looked with envy back to the sacral ambience of the middle ages, a time which witnessed, so it is conventionally held, a more peaceful and stable hierarchic system, where men's dealings with each other were more personal than they ever were to be again. The fifteenth century marked the breakdown of medieval society and the beginning of the times that culminated in the corrupt monarchy of the eighteenth century. The birth of a unified nation, with Charles VII's coronation, spelled unlimited hope for France's spiritual destiny, but marked also the start of a downward trend. It was as if France had been given a chance but had not risen fully to the task. This at least is what Claudel seems to have felt. Elisabeth's seven years of sterility, the Vercors' failure to have sons, their only grandchild being a girl, Mara's black actions, Europe's besieged state—these are perhaps all symbols of the eventual breakdown.

Why Claudel fastened on the Violaine story to present his interpretation of history is concealed in the nebulous process of artistic creation, although one can say: (1) the basic plot was in part originally inspired by his readings of the lives of the saints, many of them medieval; (2) the first two Violaine plays were relatively timeless, especially the first, which meant that the action was easily transferable to a specific age; (3) Combernon is a medieval farm[12]; (4) Claudel had a predilection for returning to old plots to present new ideas; (5) he probably associated Violaine with such real saints and/or mystics of the time as Lydwina of Schiedam (*cf.* the character Lidine in the first version), Colette of Corbie (Corbie is very near Combernon), Catherine of Sienna, Joan of Arc. Their deeds, prayers and assumption through suffering (often with ills like leprosy—*cf.* the precedent of the blind leprous Emperor of *Le Repos*) of the sins of the world are held by some as instrumental in the subsequent general recovery. A curious anachronism, but understandable both because the original plot transpires in winter and because of Claudel's attachment to that particular day, is the transfer of the coronation from July 27 (1429) to Christmas Day.

Justice plays a great role, beginning with the church to be built in honor of the fictional virgin martyr Saint Justice. God's justice encompasses one and all and everything, but more special kinds are presented: negative justice or laws and conventions, positive justice or charity. Anne, Pierre, Violaine, exemplars of the second sort, effect an amelioration in the state of the negative justice then applying to papal and kingly rule. The reverse too can be true. The interaction of the two justices is an important addition to the third Violaine play. For the poignant study of the heroine's hesitations, the beautifully expressed emotions and lessons, *L'Annonce faite à Marie* is generally thought of as Claudel's best play.

A one-act farce *Protée* followed *L'Annonce*. It is gay and witty, written somewhat in the spirit of Marivaux' *Ile des esclaves*. What astonishes about this light humorous play is the number of his serious themes Claudel was able to implant in it.

V *LE PAIN DUR*

Then, in 1913 and 1914, Claudel wrote *Le Pain dur*, the direct continuation of *L'Otage*. The second play of the trilogy takes place during the reign of Louis-Philippe—the July Monarchy. The time is about 1840. Louis, the child of Turelure and Sygne, has already had a colonial career in Africa. The plot is the most intricate of his standard-length plays. The scene is the same as in the first play, but symbolically, the crucifix is down and leaning against the wall. The personages are: Louis, bankrupt because of the failure of his African plantation; Turelure; Ali Habenichts, Jewish moneylender who has dealings with Turelure; Sichel, Ali's daughter and Turelure's mistress but in love with Louis; Lumîr, aristocratic Polish adventuress and Louis' fiancée, who had lent him the money to start up his African enterprise but now has to restore it to the treasury (from which she had taken it illegally) for a free Poland. She wants this sum, and an equal one from Turelure, in order to return Louis to solvency. Embittered with her persecuted lot as a Jewess, Sichel—Sickle, and one thinks of the cutting sound of Ysé—has a double motive for wanting to marry Louis. She discovers Lumîr will be content to get her money back and leave. Turelure does not like his son, whose debt he is being called on to pay, and who resembles both himself and Sygne too closely for comfort. He actually had caused his son's bankruptcy, which was the basic cause for the plantation's failure. Lumîr, desperate for her money, suggests to Louis that he frighten his father into repayment by aiming two guns at him, one loaded, one blank. Meanwhile, Sichel has got Turelure to protect his money from such machinations by pretending to assign it to her and her father for safekeeping. Louis fires *both* guns and it turns out *both* were loaded in the first place: treachery on both his part and Lumîr's. He misses twice, but Turelure drops dead from shock. Technically, Sichel and Ali are his heirs; however, she tears up the documents. Louis, honorably indebted to her, agrees to marry her. Lumîr the wanderer departs with her money. At the end, Louis sells Ali the bronze in the cast-aside crucifix.

Pain dur—stale bread, hard bread, ironlike bread, the iron age, the industrial revolution. This is the subject of the play. Many things have gone from bad to worse. Sygne and Georges were attached to each other, but thirty years later father and son— Turelure and Louis—hate each other viciously. Belief is dead. Society's rush to depersonalization has apocalyptically increased. That is the primary message. The nineteenth century witnessed the sanctions lifted from Jewry and also saw new, more promising attempts at freedom by the older subjugated nationalities. This helps to explain Ali, Sichel, Lumîr. Here, Claudel was more a describer than an interpreter of those times.

The play is interesting, dramatically powerful, and is an excellent transposition of a most defendable synthesis of the age it examines. Aesthetically, then, it is beautiful. Of conventionally conceived beauty it has little. Claudel, the singer of creation, found not much to sing of in those times, which had nullified any hopes that the Restoration might have engendered at its beginning. There is not even love. Lumîr, a Rimbaud figure, has earthbound ideals. Claudel wrote this play in Frankfurt and Hamburg on the brink of the First World War. There were many Jews in these two trade centers, which adds to the reasons for the presence of Ali and his daughter. This grimmest of Claudel's plays owes something to the grimness of the time when it was written. Harking back to the parricidal aspect of the 1888 *Une Mort prématurée*, one wonders if Claudel's father's death in 1913 in any way is related to Turelure's demise in *Le Pain dur*. Another similarity to that fragment is Louis' incest-like union with his father's mistress.

Before completing the play, Claudel had already begun translating the second play of the *Oresteia*. *Les Choéphores* was followed by *Les Euménides* in 1916. Between these he wrote the short *Nuit de Noël 1914*, about which the less said the better. Claudel sometimes abandoned his reason and sentiments to chauvinism and/or Catholicism. In *La Nuit de Noël 1914* the Germans, not the Allies, commit all the atrocities. In Claudel's defense, he was not a Spinoza but a poet, whose transcribed *états d'âme* do not all have to be parts of a sensible and coherent whole.

VI   *LE PERE HUMILIE*

In 1915 and 1916 he also wrote *Le Père humilié*. The humiliated father in 1869 when the play begins is the pope, who is about to lose his temporal powers. The scene is of course Rome. Louis is the self-serving French ambassador to the Vatican. Sichel is old and worn now. Pensée is their daughter; she is most beautiful, and blind. So attuned to her condition is she that she can walk in strange places among strangers without stumbling, without their realizing she cannot see: from one point of view, compensatory synesthesia. The pope figures strongly in the drama. So do his two nephews Orso and Orian, the latter also his godson. Pensée, cursed by her heritage, is without faith. She loves Orian. Both brothers love her, Orian secretly. Where Orso is a more earthy individual whose heart and mind have no great vocation to transcend the ordinary, Orian is not: If he fixes his capacities for a higher love on the chances for a physical and spiritual relationship with Pensée, he knows his soul will be in danger. His true vocation is elsewhere. Ironically, Pensée is his spiritual mate, but can be no other sort. Orso, another Miles Standish, unsuspectingly asks Orian to speak for him to Pensée. From the beginning of their interview they sense the truth. Finally, Pensée:

> Ah, be still, my beloved! and, the word you are going to say, keep it for me until another time, when body and soul separate!
> Be still, and that word which is not made for earth, that soundless word that you're saying to me, look, I've read it on your lips! (I, 3; X, 237)

Typically, the sensitive Pensée has absorbed Orian's problems. Only at the very end of the scene does she tell him she is blind.

Orso and Orian bring their mutual love for Pensée before their uncle the pope, who has just been talking sadly to his confidant, a humble Minorite, about the state of Christianity:

> They say they're not thirsty; they say this isn't a spring; they say it's not water; they say it's not what they think a spring and water are like; they say there's no such thing as water (II, 1; 242).

Each brother wishes to give up Pensée to the other. The pope, aware of the fine points of Orian's dilemma (Pensée now is too), suggests Orso marry her. Orian leaves for Africa and Orso ultimately becomes engaged to Pensée, believing that time will cool past ardors.

The beginning of the Franco-Prussian War one year later finds Orian back in Rome. He and Orso are to go off to fight for France. The frenzy of the period weakens the resolve of both the real lovers. Furthermore, Pensée reminds Orian of the papacy's debt to her, meaning the time when Sygne protected another pope. They consummate their love physically. Before he leaves they see each other once more, hardly in their right minds.

A few months later in January 1871, Pensée, pregnant with Orian's child, waits in vain for a letter from him. Orso arrives to

90 PAUL CLAUDEL

apprise her of his brother's last repentant moments on the battle-field. Orian is thus absolved. She and Orso will marry only in form, in order to give a name to the child.

The bond between the star-crossed lovers is overwhelmingly beautiful, in itself, and for its inexorable impossibility. Why, in the author's terms, must God in His infinite wisdom bring just the two people together who can spell each other's doom? Because they also spell each other's salvation. Orian raises Pensée to his height (thus effectively repaying the old papal debt); she is the agent of his sacrifice, his suffering, and his ultimate redemption. Sin too plays its Claudelian role.

The names of the three younger protagonists add much to the story. Pensée (thought, pansy) for a blind person of such extreme sensitivity ignites many rich allusions. Orso is bearlike, and one also thinks of Ursus Major, the Big Bear (or Big Dipper). Orian is like the handsome warrior who became the constellation Orion, also called Saint Jacques (James), which visits both hemispheres. The brothers' names thus strengthen the extra-worldly ambience.

The predominance of the *Partage* theme in *Le Père humilié* makes one look again at the three major plays written between these two. The theme had not been dormant dramatically since 1905. Violaine, Sygne, Lumîr all represent it in one way or another. Why is Rome the setting for the third part of the trilogy? Many obvious explanations spring from the preceding plots and Claudel's general frames of reference. Perhaps less obvious ones are that Claudel himself was in Rome in 1915 and 1916, that the two *Ville*'s had already taken place in the France of about that period, possibly calling for a setting outside his country in order to relieve the "competition." Perhaps, too, Claudel's diatribes against the nineteenth century naturally centered on his own country, which he knew best. Changing the scene to Rome allowed him to inveigh more clearly against the faults of all Christendom. Furthermore, wartime might have been no time to seem to concentrate his attacks on his own country.

One may wonder where Claudel meant to leave his audience at the end of the third play. *L'Echange* has certainly a no more resolved ending, but these three plays are supposed to depict the fruits of the Revolution, which were not all bad. The older Claudel got, the more he thought this. Where is, not the happy ending, but the possibility of one? Surely not in Pensée's womb. Very late in life, Claudel described the never-written play that would have made the series a tetralogy:

All I know is that the new play would have centered on a very old Pensée, let's say seventy, who would have had a role . . . which would have combined in herself the explanation of all those past troubles, as well as an opening into the future. . . . It was only in a very different form, and which had no historical contact with the three plays, that I later found what can be called a solution, a consummation of the Trilogy in *Le Soulier de satin*. . . .[13]

That is one sort of tetralogy. Another can be suggested, because of the philosophical relationship between *L'Annonce faite à Marie* and *L'Otage*. At any rate, the trilogy does not add up to the non-fragmentary conclusion envisaged by Claudel in his 1908 letter to Frizeau. And perhaps it is better off for it, life situations not being so cut and dried.

In 1917 Claudel wrote *L'Ours et la lune*, a one-act play half of which is puppetry. In it, the moon is an intermediary between spatially separated people, and magically changes some of them into other individuals, a phenomenon that had already happened in *Protée*. Two choreographies followed, *L'Homme et son désir* of the same year, *La Femme et son ombre* of 1922. They mark of course a new departure. Early in 1917 Claudel had sailed for Rio de Janeiro and the post of plenipotentiary minister, accompanied by Darius Milhaud for secretary. Francis Jammes had brought the two together in 1912. Milhaud composed the music for the first ballet as the beginning of what was to prove to be a fruitful collaboration.[14]

VII   LE SOULIER DE SATIN

Claudel spent from 1919 to 1924 on his most ambitious dramatic work, *Le Soulier de satin*, grandiose in scope and length. During most of this period he was Ambassador to Japan. The great 1923 Tokyo earthquake destroyed many of his manuscripts, including the entire third *journée* of the play, which he had to rewrite from memory.

One has to think back to the time when Claudel brought Saint Thomas' *Summas* with him to China at the end of the century. *Le Soulier* is certainly his own summa. Intricately plotted, three

92

times the length of one of his regular efforts, it would require many pages to be dealt with adequately. Only sparse ideas of the plot and meaning can be provided here. *Le Soulier* draws together many themes, techniques and ideas to be found in Claudel's preceding plays. Puppetry is employed; here too the moon unites those far apart geographically; the *Partage* theme prevails above all others; pairs of individuals are destined for telling encounters on earth. In addition, there are many Japanese theatrical touches.

Le Soulier synthesizes from a Catholic viewpoint the age that brought Luther, but also sent missionaries across the globe. The Renaissance is a symbol of Christ's conquest of the universe. Its meaning, then, applies to all times, especially perhaps to those in which it was written. *Le Soulier* is optimistic. The play focuses on the year 1600 and the Spanish occupation of the New World, but is anachronistic to the extreme. Remember how history is rewritten in *L'Otage* and *L'Annonce*. The new play outdoes them by far: It even "time-machines" modern real-life characters, not to speak of a bicycle, back to the Renaissance.

Prouhèze is married to Pélage. She and Rodrigue (a former novice!: recall Turelure, Claudel himself) fall in love. Her husband dispatches her, with Camille as her lieutenant, to protect the African fortress of Mogador. Camille is a renegade. Pélage is aware that both Camille and Rodrigue love Prouhèze. Mogador is the test he sets his wife. A Renaissance Rimbaud, Rodrigue tries to get Prouhèze to leave the fortress and go with him, but she refuses. Apparently she has been strengthened by the Virgin, to whom she has plighted her spiritual purity, using as an offering one of her satin slippers. Hence the title. Claudel once said the idea of the slipper came from a novel he had read twenty years before writing the play, while living in China.[15] Then too, he may have met the real Ysé during a shipboard game of hunt-the-slipper, a memory that could have flashed to mind when he re-encountered the real-life Ysé while writing the play.[16] Whether none, one, or both incidents served as influence here matters little, since *Le Soulier* is so inarguably a spiritualized version of *Partage de midi*. Endowed with Orian's and Pensée's wisdom, or Ysé's, Rodrigue leaves for the Americas, where as viceroy he performs brilliantly for the King of Spain. Pélage dies; Prouhèze sends for Rodrigue by a letter that takes *ten years* to reach its destinee.

Meanwhile, she and Camille wed and have a child, Sept-Epées. When Rodrigue finally arrives at Mogador, it is on the point of being blown up (Mesa's and Ysé's dwelling at the end of *Partage*) by the Arabs. Prouhèze rejects Rodrigue's pleas to save her with oblique *Partage*-like reasons that Rodrigue fails to grasp. She entrusts him with Sept-Epées, into whose great physical resemblance to him one can read God's reward for their continence (Violaine's reward). Prouhèze dies. Ultimately, Rodrigue loses favor and is reduced to dire poverty. He has lost a leg (Rimbaud) in combat. Sept-Epées, daughter of the King of Naples and Musique, marries Juan d'Autriche. The latter had been present at Rodrigue's and Prouhèze's first encounter. Finally, Rodrigue becomes a porter in a convent. Only then, without a single earthly attachment, does he fully understand how the adventure of his life has been directed by the divine scheme of things. His great love was not for this world but for another. The last line of the play is "Release of captured souls!" (IV, 11; XII, 339)

One cannot begin to give pertinent or beautiful quotations, or to go into the plot's finer intricacies. There is something for everybody in the sense that any given individual must be drawn emotionally to certain ones among the play's countless top qualities. Most effective is the feeling of oneness imparted. Spain and America are presented in God's same "time"; ten years pass in God's same "space." In this ambience, anachronisms cease to be and guardian angels become believable. The sense of the title-page epigraphs, *etiam peccata* and *Deus escreve direito por linhas tortas*, comes across richly. The former is more linked to the love between Rodrigue and Prouhèze, the latter to the ups and downs of Christendom's fate during the Renaissance and across all time. The two currents are intermingled. Rodrigue's perfect realization of the meaning of his life in terms of the universe, that is, of his role in the universal analogy, is not completely distinct from Christendom's role. Claudel's epiphanal dream has not transpired on earth, at least not yet. While looking back at the Renaissance, *Le Soulier* also looks forward, to the dream's accomplishment. Thus, in Claudel's terms the play redounds with optimism and hope.

Seeing and reading *Le Soulier de satin* are indispensable complements. Its poetry and profundity cannot be thoroughly appreciated in the theatrical experience alone; only a careful reading can fix the plot exactly, whose complications, plus the large cast, remind one of the first *Ville*. (This is not to say that *La Ville* is as deserving of the effort.) On the other hand, the mind's eye cannot sufficiently recompose the grandiose pageantry of such as the Cadiz scene (II, 1), with all its hustle-bustle of men and commerce oriented toward the New World. Clearly contrary-to-fact scenes dealing with, say, the supernatural profit from staging, not so much to make them credible (indeed the motive may not be that at all) as to enhance the inspiring intention behind their creation. Not just for its length, *Le Soulier de satin* is Claudel's greatest play. And if *L'Annonce faite à Marie* is not his best play, then *Le Soulier* is.

The sinful love in *Le Père humilié* makes one reflect again on *Partage de midi* and the three interim plays. *Le Soulier* encourages similar reflections. In *Un Amour de Swann*, the hero's love for Odette reaches agonizing heights just before its termination. Closer to home, the fourth of Claudel's *Cinq Grandes Odes* (1900-1908) recounts a similar last-ditch struggle before the final resolution of that long work's *Partage* theme. In this vein, *Le Père humilié* depicts physical love's last great resurgence, and *Le Soulier*, whose two star-crossed lovers never sin, continues the parallel through the cosmic resolution of the "problem." From a different standpoint *Le Soulier*, the Trilogy, and *L'Annonce* comprise a sort of historical pentateuch, of which the last-written play, treating of so much more than the Renaissance, is clearly the capstone.

Before and while writing *Le Soulier*, Claudel felt it would represent his adieu to the theater. This explains why it is a summa, in regard to life, to his own life, to his theatrical career. Love and all existence are resolved in the play; by the time of its composition Claudel had attained a supreme post-*Tête d'or* and post-*Partage* serenity. He already knew his Shakespeare. As further homework he read Calderon and Lope de Vega, though by no means for the first time. They were his type of playwright. He called the four unequally lengthed acts "journées" ("days"), after the "jornadas" of Spanish plays. Through *Le Soulier*, Claudel had written eight superb plays: the first *Echange*, the second *Jeune Fille Violaine*, and all six of his second period, which clearly marked his theatrical apogee. As noted, the five historical plays were written then. But the unifying factor of all six is the combined *etiam peccata* and *Partage* thematic content.

C. THIRD PERIOD 1925-1955

La Parabole du festin or *Le Festin de la sagesse* (1924); *Protée*, 2nd v. (1926); *Le Livre de Christophe Colomb* (1927); *Sous le rempart d'Athènes* (1927); *Jeanne d'Arc au bûcher* (1934); *L'Annonce faite à Marie*, new Act IV (1938); *L'Histoire de Tobie et de Sara*, 1st v. (1938); *Le Jet de pierre* (1938); *Le Soulier de satin*, abridged v. (1944); *Le Père humilié*, 2nd v. (1945); *La Lune à la recherche d'elle-même* (1947); *L'Annonce faite à Marie*, 4th Violaine play (1948); *Partage de midi*, 2nd v. (1948), 3rd v. (1948-1949); *Tête d'or*, incomplete 3rd v. (1949); *Le Ravissement de Scapin* (1949); *L'Echange*, 2nd v. (1950-1951); *L'Histoire de Tobie et de Sara*, 2nd v. (1952).

The quantity of third period works so belies their importance that a change in approach is warranted here. By 1924 Claudel had finished evolving as a dramatist. Other considerations had taken hold. Because of this, only the following merit more than cursory attention: *Le Livre de Christophe Colomb*, *Jeanne d'Arc au bûcher*, *L'Histoire de Tobie et de Sara*, *Partage de midi*, *L'Echange*.

La Parabole du festin, which schematizes an oratorio, belongs chronologically to the second but fits better in the third, "biblical" period. Psalmlike, it combines the spirit of the Old and the New Testaments. At the same time, it is fashioned after the Japanese No plays. The second *Protée* is inferior to the first. The plot of both concerns the Helen of Troy myth, but part of the second's reorientation is to fill in the elliptical references of the first. Generally clarification is fine, but not so when, in the first place, the basic plot is so referential. The explanations bore. *Sous le rempart d'Athènes* should figure prominently in any study of transposition as a feature of Claudel's art. This short play with an ancient Greek setting sums up Marcelin Berthelot, the father of Philippe, Claudel's Quai d'Orsay protector. The Act IV variant of *L'Annonce* eliminates one of the two somewhat cloying coincidences. In the earlier play, both Pierre de Craon and Anne Vercors return to Combernon just after Mara has fatally assaulted her sister. The variant has only Anne Vercors return. This may still be one coincidence too many, but probably not: Claudel's theater represents more or less of a compromise between verisimilitude and divine intervention. The new Act IV also removes some of the catechistic and poetic aspects of the original. The skit *Le Jet de*

pierre transposes the workings of a poet's mind while he is
asleep. It is a dramatization of Claudel's *Cantate à trois voix*
(1911-1912). The abridged version of *Le Soulier de satin* is just
that. The second *Père humilié* perhaps should not be designated
as a version, in the sense the word has been used up to here,
because it is little different from the first. *La Lune à la recherche
d'elle-même* is a radio version of *L'Endormie*. The 1948 *Annonce
faite à Marie* is supposedly an acting rendition of the first, but
the 1911 play, with the Act IV variant, is the one usually produced. In any case, the 1911 and 1948 forms are not essentially
different. There are thus four full-length Violaine plays. The
1938 variant makes a sort of fifth. In addition, Henri Mondor has
discovered parts of a *Jeune Fille Violaine* which either precedes
or directly follows the first version.[17] Thus, it can be held that
there are *six* Violaine plays. The third *Tête d'or* is extremely inchoate. *Le Ravissement de Scapin* is an adaptation of Molière's
play.

   The libretto of the multi-tableau'd *Livre de Christophe Colomb*
was Claudel's first theatrical effort after he had turned away from
drama in the strict sense. The musical score was composed by
Darius Milhaud, who had, since the 1917 *Homme et son désir*,
set several of Claudel's works to music after the fact, notably the
three plays of the *Oresteia*. *Colomb* was their first total collaboration on a long work. The text is ambivalent. It has been played
both as a pure opera, and as a play with Milhaud's background
music.

   Since by 1927 Claudel thought he had exhausted the regular
play form as a vehicle for what he had to say, and since the huge
shadow of *Le Soulier de satin* looms over it, *Le Livre de Christophe Colomb* is important and interesting as an opera but is relatively eclipsed as a play. It has the major themes, but none is stated
in a vitally new way. Tableau XV, entitled "Recruiting for the cara-
velles," is set in Cadiz and echoes the similar scene in *Le Soulier*.
The opera begins at the end of the hero's life. He is seventy-five
years old and in chains. Now Rodrigue, before being a porter, had
been a slave. So one realizes that he already was a symbol of Columbus' fate. This is not the only "second-hand" feature of *Colomb*.
Reminiscent of Prouhèze's slipper is the ring Queen Isabella offers
up for Columbus' success. *Colomb* has one great advantage over
Le Soulier: Of the two historical pageants, the former is naturally

more accessible because its plot line stems directly from history, on which the chorus, furthermore, frequently expands.

I *JEANNE D'ARC AU BUCHER*

The oratorio *Jeanne d'Arc au bûcher* (*Joan at the stake*) was written in 1934; Arthur Honneger composed the music. Claudel had been asked to produce the libretto by a group of *license* candidates at the Sorbonne. After an initial refusal, he surprised them two weeks later with the completed manuscript. It is his best-known musical collaboration. The times helped the work. War was close. France had to consolidate the forces represented by the traditional values. The last words of the oratorio are: "No one has a greater love than to give his life for those he loves" (sc. 11; XIV, 105). As one might expect, and as in *Colomb*, the oratorio depends on generally known features of the central character's life. People come and go before the chained Maid of Orleans, reliving their moments with her. Apart from musical values, and from the fact that one is a pageant, the other is static, both opera and oratorio are similar in inspiration and execution. One could say that both are really pageants of the mind.

II *L'HISTOIRE DE TOBIE ET DE SARA*

Claudel's 1938 morality play, *L'Histoire de Tobie et de Sara*, slightly retouched ten years later, is his best latter-day theatrical work. Originally he had planned for music to be essential to it, as with *Colomb* and *Jeanne*, but he rightly changed his mind. As played, *Tobie et Sara* is a dramatic work fully able to stand alone, with or without the incidental music that sometimes accompanies it. It is an adaptation of a little-known biblical story, or, as Claudel would have it, "parable." If it is not one inarguably in the Old Testament, it certainly is one in his rendition. Toby the Young leaves Ninevah and his parents Ann and the blind Toby the Elder for Media, where he must recover the money his father had lent to Rachel. Her daughter Sara has seen seven husbands to the grave before any one of them could consummate his marriage with her. She is being saved by God for Toby. As in *L'Annonce*, the persons involved seem to both know and not know such information. The upshot is that with parts of a fish Azarias (the Archangel Raphael in disguise) causes him to catch, Toby frees Sara of her curse and cures his father's blindness. The predestined lovers wed.

The old themes of destiny, blindness, Toby as a Rimbaud figure, and so forth abound in a tensionless ambience. More tranquilly here even than in *Le Soulier* did Claudel hold forth on love. Where *Le Soulier* goes about resolving the problem, in *Tobie et Sara*, a work of serene old age, there is nothing to resolve. Steeped in the Bible, Claudel gave his play an authenticity of miraculous sacredness that is nothing like the more intellectually conceived impossibilities of *Le Soulier*. In only one other play (besides *Le Soulier* and *Tobie et Sara*) does the supernatural intervene: *L'Annonce*. Even in *Tobie et Sara* one feels more that Claudel would have liked things to be this way than that he believed they were. Yet it would go against the meaning of parable to insist too much on authenticity, for Claudel was an anti-literalist who saw God's meaning in all things. Simply, in 1938 he was authentically at home in the Bible, and this reinforcement makes of *Tobie et Sara* surely one of his best plays.

III   *Serenity as a Hindrance*

The second and third *Partage de midi* are not very different. They are both quite eviscerated, the third more than the second. The second *Echange*, written about sixty years after the first, is similarly much less physical. The second *Partage* is a compromise between the old play and the totally rewritten one that Claudel wanted Jean-Louis Barrault to put on in 1948. The third *Partage* is actually that new rewriting, plus a few additions. It would seem that there could just as well have been a third *Echange* of this type.

The new versions found Claudel in the state of biblical serenity that gave *Tobie et Sara* all its strength but sapped theirs. For example, the end of the third version of *Partage* is a ten-page sermon by the dying Ysé and Mesa on the meaning of love in this world. At least the third *Partage* has the integrity of the unity absent in the second. The turbulent freshness of the sinful love behind it is more aggravating for being there one moment, absent the next. The 1950-1951 *Echange* suffers from this second malady. Ysé the sinner-turned-preacher is now paralleled by Marthe the victim—the youthful Claudel in a hostile foreign clime—turned into Marthe the shrew: the aged Claudel impatient with sin. Louis leaves without his money; Pollock refuses to pick it up; Lechy is given pleasant things to say. All the same, the four are left much of their old characters. The triple whitewash and the change in Marthe are understandable in terms of Claudel's different psyche. But they are not, in a plot where two different psyches create oscillating characterizations. In a preface to the latter *Echange* Claudel explained clearly what he was about: Money is "the possibility of something else"; Pollock "the celebrant" of change and exchange; Louis is the "last representative of a condemned race" who "sought out across the Ocean the only one, Marthe, a woman, who had the power as well as the vocation to save him. . . . Marthe is reason, virtue," and Lechy is "Imagination, the Unknown . . ." (VIII, 89-90). The trouble simply was that the attempt at a modern-day parable was contaminated by the conflict between two influences, the first *Echange* as opposed to his usual method of creation.[18]

IV *The Dramatist Reviewed*

To repeat, with *Le Soulier de satin* Claudel planned to give up writing plays since he thought he had said all he could in the genre. His long list of post-*Soulier* theatrical works does not contradict too much his earlier intention. Many of the works are short, or not as dramatic as the pieces before the mid-twenties. Two, *Colomb* and *Jeanne*, are libretti. Two plays, the second *Annonce* and *Soulier*, are more scenic adaptations than proper second versions. As for the two late versions of *Partage* and the second *Echange*, these are really not as concerned with the dramatic process in the way their previous versions had been; for the last two versions of *Partage* also are parabolizations. Claudel of course did backtrack from his euphorious old age to try to make them successful. But his mind and heart were elsewhere, with other, greater preoccupations that sapped his dramatic capacities. Which leads to the paradox of *Le Livre de Tobie et de Sara*, whose extra-dramatic motivations make it one of Claudel's great dramatic works. At any rate, from one point of view Claudel never did attempt, with all his powers, to write another dramatic play like any of those of his second, golden, period.

For Claudel the dramatist means essentially Claudel of the six plays from *Partage* through *Soulier*, from 1905 through 1924. The years before were preparatory; during them his already matured poetic gifts gradually fashioned themselves into the dramatic mold. In the years following, his orientation had changed. Exceptions to this definition are *L'Echange* and the second *Jeune Fille Violaine* of the "training" period, and the post-*Soulier Tobie et Sara*. On these nine plays Claudel's position as a great lyric dramatist rests firmly.

CHAPTER 4

Poetry

ANYBODY would turn over in his grave, especially a sometime germanophobe, if he were called a stomachic-apocalyptic-philosophic - prosodic - analogizing - hypersensitive - chauvinistic-transposing-impressionable-iconoclastic-Catholic-catholic-influenceable-autobiographical-natural-primordial-joyous-experimental writer. Fortunately, Claudel does not have to be so described here before one describes his poetry because the foregoing chapters announce that he is all this. In his essay "Introduction à un poème sur Dante" (1921), he wrote:

> The object of poetry isn't really, as is often said, dreams, illusions, ideas. It's that holy reality, given once and forever, in the center of which we are placed. It's the universe of invisible things. It's all that watches us and which we watch. All that is God's work, which constitutes the inexhaustible material of the recitals and songs, as much of the greatest poet as of the smallest bird (*Positions et propositions I*; XV, 94).

Dante is an imperial or catholic poet for three reasons: his inspiration, his intelligence, his catholicity (92-94). Elsewhere, Claudel wrote that the advantages of religious art are threefold: the praise it offers up to the deity, the authenticity of the expression or of the words it is graced with, and the authenticity of the drama it presents.[1] Still elsewhere: "We go from visible things to invisible things, not always as if from the effect to the cause, but as if from the sign to the thing signified, and not so much along the roads of logic as along those of analogy."[2] And this is how Saint Paul described the vertical analogy: "While we look not at the things which are seen, but at the things which are not seen; for the things which are seen are temporal; but the things which are not seen are eternal" (*II Corinthians;* 4: 18).

Claudel was intrigued by Mallarmé's question, applicable to

101

any phenomenon: "What does that mean?" But he added the provision: "What does God mean that that means?" He sought out his analogies as did Baudelaire, listened as did Mallarmé, included considerations for his God, and produced the *verset claudélien*, the psychological breath. *Art poétique* (1900-1904) and "Réflexions et propositions sur le vers français" (1925; *Positions et propositions I*) are his own most thorough elaborations on his own poetics.

The problem as to which is Claudel's best genre is additionally puzzling in that all his theater is poetry as well. Furthermore, his less superior theater contains superior poetry, notably the first *Ville*, the second *Tête d'or*, *Le Repos du septième jour*, the last two *Partage de midi*, and the second *Echange*. The broad and Claudelian conception of poetry also confuses the issue. This chapter is limited to a survey of Claudel's non-dramatic poetry in poetic form, to his prose-poetry, and to his translations of poetry: The last category includes what is better described as his reactions to, rather than his translations of, many of the Psalms.

Formal Poetry and Prose-Poems[3]

Premiers Vers (1886-1900); *Vers d'exil* (1895); *Connaissance de l'Est* (1895-1905); *Cinq Grandes Odes*, followed by *Processional pour saluer le siècle nouveau* (1900-1908); *La Cantate à trois voix* (1911-1912); *Corona benignitatis anni Dei* (1887-1914); *La Messe là-bas* and *L'Offrande du temps* (1917); *Feuilles de saints* (1910-1925); *Poèmes de guerre* (1915-1944); *Visages radieux* (1927-1944); *Poésies diverses* (1925-1950).

I PREMIERS VERS (FIRST POEMS)

These are six poems gathered together for the first time in 1950 in volume one of the *OEuvres complètes*, four of them never having been printed before. They are loyal offerings to traditional prosody. "Celui-là seul saura sourire" (1897) is a sonnet in the style of Mallarmé and dedicated to the master, which begins:

> Only he may smile, if so has concurred
> The Muse herself, his schoolmistress and Mother,
> She forms, opening to him letter and Grammar,
> His lip to the exact line and the absolute Word.

Celui-là seul saura sourire, s'il a plu
A la Muse elle-même, institutrice et Mère,
De former, lui ouvrant la Lettre et la Grammaire,
Sa lèvre au vers exact et au Mot absolu (13).

Very interesting autobiographically is "Pour la messe des hommes dernier sacrifice d'amour!" ("For the mass of men last sacrifice of love!"). Dated August 30, 1886, it is halfway between the influence of Rimbaud and the return to belief. Christ monologs in all but the last of the poem's twelve quatrains, and it would seem to provide a glimpse of Claudel's conversion-in-the-making. True to tradition, the poem is in properly alternating alexandrines.

These first efforts show an able enough practitioner of the old prosody. They are none of them startlingly good, but after all most were written when he was only in his late teens. Externally his dramatic poetry, already in free verse, probably provided any needed release from the rules according to his own account he often repeated his personal inability to fit himself into a classical mold. Which came first, his general, but not universal, loathing of the alexandrine or his weakness in respect to it? This is an easy question to answer but it is neither a fair one, nor even pertinent.

II *VERS D'EXIL*

Claudel probably wrote all these eleven pieces (one unfinished) in 1895 in China, just before launching into the prose-poems of *Connaissance de l'Est*, which in turn are the forerunners of *Art poétique*. The *Vers d'exil* are formally traditional, mostly in quatrains. There are three *idées maîtresses*. The strongest is quiescent hope for a vocation, implicit in the title-opening-line of the eighth: "Take back the talent you gave me" ("Reprenez le talent que vous m'avez donné"). The weakest central idea is the nostalgia suggested by the collection's title. "Now I'm alone under a new sky" ("Maintenant je suis seul sous un soleil nouveau") says the fourth line of the first poem. The other theme in some ways duplicates the first. It concerns Claudel's interest in his own act of poetic creation—but from which he wants to be separated if his call to the priesthood be genuine. The fifth poem begins:

Man's noise, steps, cries, laughs, calls, front,
Back, songs, loves, quarrels, bargains, words!
I want to blind you, people moving within me!
Quiet, sonorous spirit! Silence, mad voices!

Bruit de l'homme, pas, cris, rires, appels, devant,
Derrière, chants, amours, rixes, marchés, paroles!
Je te veux aveugler, ô peuple en moi mouvant!
Tais-toi, sonore espirit! Etouffez-vous, voix folles! (35)

These poems suffer in stemming mostly from Claudel's alter-
ego, that is, the Cébès or the Lambert de Besme lurking inside
him. It may be possible for some individuals to be dynamic in
their quiescence, but it was not so for Claudel. That may even
help explain why, not much later on, his vocation was found to
be lacking. Also, the form was too containing for someone already
a past master of free-verse expression. The *Vers d'exil* are perhaps
more experimental than not. In any case, they are extremely rich
in autobiography:

> You have vanquished me, my beloved! My enemy,
> You took from my hands my weapons one by one.
> And now I have no longer a single defense.
> And here I am naked before you, Friend.

> Tu m'as vaincu, mon bien-aimé! Mon ennemi,
> Tu m'as pris dans mes mains mes armes une à une.
> Et maintenant je n'ai plus de défense aucune.
> Et voici que je suis nu devant vous, Ami! (38)

III *CONNAISSANCE DE L'EST*[4]

Fifty-three of these short pieces were written between 1895
and 1901. The other nine were composed from 1901 to 1905.
Some of the sixty-two may not be held to be prose-poems at all,
but for convenience the entire work is considered here. In a related vein, a few parts of *L'Oiseau noir dans le soleil levant*
(1923-1927) are prose-poems, but since the work is predominat-
ingly prose it is relegated *in toto* to the following chapter. In
these two collections nearly all Claudel's prose-poetry is to be
found.

Connaissance means knowledge or acquaintance(ship), but
perhaps a more faithful translation would be *Meaning of the
East*, referring back to Mallarmé's seminal question. At any rate,
this book illustrates superbly the idea that all of Claudel's work
is poetry. What its poems share with his other genres is the
higher presence in whatever subject is at hand. *Connaissance*
must be read aloud. Some of the poems get so involved with de-

scription or ideas that they are more essay than poem. Here though is a paragraph which, paradoxically, for its very prosiness, can show the poetic common denominator of all the sixty-two parts:

The countryside is a vast cemetery. Everywhere, coffins; hillocks covered with withered reeds, and, in the dry grass, rows of little stone posts, mitred statues, lions, indicate old sepulchers. The guilds, the rich, have built edifices surrounded by trees and hedges. I pass between an animal refuge and a well stuffed with corpses of girl-children whose parents have got rid of them. It was capped when it was filled; another will have to be dug.

La campagne est un vaste cimetière. Partout, des cercueils; des monticules couverts de roseaux flétris, et, dans l'herbe sèche, des rangées de petits pieux en pierre, des statues mitrées, des lions, indiquent les sépultures antiques. Les corporations, les riches, ont bâti des édifices entourés d'arbres et de haies. Je passe entre un hospice pour les animaux et un puits rempli de cadavres de petites filles dont leurs parents se sont débarrassés. On l'a bouché, une fois comble; il en faudra creuser un autre ("La Pagode"; 15).

The denominator is the aesthetic quality transcending any prose situation present, in this case transcending an enumerative description. Bypassing the vowels, consonants, syllables of the original French—the aspects of Claudel's art hardest to "bring over" to another language—one can readily appreciate from the English the aesthetic orientation of the passage. The walk through a stark landscape is transposed by a gait-like series of sentences that are shorter even than the punctuation signifies. The poetic eye seeks out complementary details such as withered reeds, dry grass. Care is taken to avoid repetition of "and," or of the verb "to be." There are the macabre ironies: a live-animal refuge in the face of human death; the rich perpetuating their richness in the form of their tombs; the next children's well must now be dug. Over and above prosody, Claudel's editorial comment is even here present: preference for the old; stress on the unchristianity (and bourgeois Christianity?) of the scene; criticism of the complacent bourgeois. If a relatively prosaic passage can contain so many aesthetic and/or Claudelian elements, one can imagine the achievements of the richer ones.

The nominal subjects of the sixty-odd poems are diffuse enough to defy categorization. Some have nothing to do directly with the Far East, but were simply written there. For example, "Proposition sur la lumière" ("Proposition on light") is concerned with painting theories. Others stress travel itself more than the Orient —"Villes," "Pensée en mer" ("Thought on the high seas"), "Dissolution," "Le Promeneur" ("The stroller"). Some recount Eastern customs and legends—"La Cloche" ("The bell"), "Fête des morts le septième mois ("Feast of the dead in the seventh month"), "La Délivrance d'Amaterasu." Some describe objectively exotic places or things: "Pagode," "Le Cocotier" ("The coconut tree"). Others purport to be purely artistic exercises. The most anthologized piece of *Connaissance* is one of these, "Le Porc" ("The pig"), and it is a good instrument for showing how deceiving appearances can be. "Le Porc" begins:

I shall paint here the image of the Pig.
It's a solid animal and all of a piece; no joints, no neck, it shoots forward like a plowshare. Jolting along on its four dumpy hams, it's a moving snout on the lookout. The pig applies its pumplike body to every odor it detects and sucks it in. And if it has found the proper hole, it wallows in it enormously.

Je peindrai ici l'image du Porc.
C'est une bête solide et tout d'une pièce; sans jointure et sans cou, ça fonce en avant comme un soc. Cahotant sur ses quatre jambons trapus, c'est une trompe en marche qui quête, et toute odeur qu'il sent, y appliquant son corps de pompe, il l'ingurgite. Que s'il a trouvé le trou qu'il faut, il s'y vautre avec énormité (69).

Later:

Gourmand, lecher! if I present you this model, admit it: you're not completely satisfied. Neither does the body suffice unto itself, nor is the doctrine taught us in vain. "Don't apply only the eye to get truth, but all that which is unreservedly yourself." Happiness is our duty and our patrimony. A certain perfect possession is *granted.*
—But meeting a sow like the one that gave presages to Aeneus always seems prophetic to me, a political emblem. Her side is darker than the hills one sees through the rain, and when she lies down, nursing her battalion of young boars trampling over her legs, she seems to me the living image of those mountains milked by the clusters of villages attached to their torrents; she is no less massive, no less deformed.
Don't let me forget to mention that pig's blood is used as a gold-fixative.

Gourmand, paillard! si je vous présente ce modèle, avouez-le: quelque chose manque à votre satisfaction. Ni le corps ne se suffit à lui-même, ni la doctrine qu'il nous enseigne n'est vaine. "N'applique point à la vérité l'oeil seul, mais tout cela sans réserve qui est toi-même." Le bonheur est notre devoir et notre patrimoine. Une certaine possession parfaite est *donnée*.

—Mais telle que celle qui fournit à Enée des présages, la rencontre d'une truie me paraît toujours augurale, un emblème politique. Son flanc est plus obscur que les collines qu'on voit au travers de la pluie, et quand elle se couche, donnant à boire au bataillon de marcassins qui lui marche entre les jambes, elle me paraît l'image même de ces monts qui traient les grappes de villages attachées à leurs torrents, non moins massive et non moins difforme.

Je n'omets pas que le sang de cochon sert à fixer l'or (70).

As in the previous passage, partial reality leads to more complete reality. Resemblances between all things spring from their relationships in a single unity. This unity is under God. The profane leads to the sacred, the visible to the invisible. These and the ever-present prosodic considerations make of the sixty-two prose-poems of *Connaissance d l'Est* an organic whole that holds its own with efforts in the same genre by Aloysius Bertrand, Baudelaire, Rimbaud.

IV CINQ GRANDES ODES

Had he written only this work, Claudel would be a major poet. Before the composition of the *Odes,* a littérateur who was to become a good friend and steady correspondant, André Suarès, set him on Pindar, which encounter may have transfused a certain element into this five-part poem.[5] Since its writing coincides with the love affair, one knows beforehand that the latter is a central theme. As the prospect of a humble quadruped led Claudel's mind to a mountainside, then (this is understood) to the God beyond both, so his experience with Ysé underwent various artistic transpositions. Critics generally see *Partage de midi* as the foremost expression of the affair. This is right, but *Cinq Grandes Odes* is not far behind. At one time Claudel thought he would be writing four odes; later on, six. More accidentally than not, he ended with five. That figure is the same as the number of acts in a classical play, and the similarity does not end there. Accidentally or not, *Cinq Grandes Odes* is a sort of play whose plot parallels fairly closely, in exposition, development, false resolution, final resolution, that of *Partage de midi*. Yet, there are additional layers, but here too one of them echoes *Partage*: the rejected vocation of the poem's protagonist. A third theme is the presentation of an *ars poetica*. There are other, less important, ones.

I. "Les Muses." Referring to an actual sarcophagus in the Louvre figuring them, the poet calls on "The Nine Muses, and in the middle Terpsichore!/I recognize you, Maenad! I recognize you, Sibyl!" ("Les Neuf Muses, et au milieu Terpsichore!/Je te reconnais, Ménade! Je te reconnais, Sibylle!"; 51). They are all examined in the light of their contributions to the protagonist's art. This is especially Claudelian in that poetry here encompasses the domain of all the Muses. By accident or intent Mnemosyne, goddess of memory and another of the Muses, is substituted for Calliope, the Muse of eloquence.

Passages on the art of poetry abound. Here is a key one on scansion:

... Oh poet, you wouldnt sing well
   What you have to sing if you didn't sing in measure.
   But your voice is necessary to the choir when your turn has come to take your part.
   Oh grammarian in my poems! Don't look for the way, look for the center! measure, enclose the space enclosed between these solitary lamps!

... O poëte, tu ne chanterais pas bien
   Ton chant si tu ne chantais en mesure.
   Mais ta voix est nécessaire au choeur quand ton tour est venu de prendre ta partie.
   O grammairien dans mes vers! Ne cherche point le chemin, cherche le centre! mesure, comprends l'espace compris entre ces feux solitaires!
   (58)

Thus the protagonist's poetry is scanned, but not traditionally, and a grammarian's logic suffers the danger of remaining at the periphery of the message, which is the singing of God's creation.

As for the protagonist, naturally it seems his vocation is to be a poet. But is that all? Is it his highest calling? Or is being a poet being landlocked, as was Mallarmé?

I have found the secret; I know how to speak; if I want, I can
tell you
What each thing *means.*
I'm initiated to the silence; there's the inexhaustible living cere-
mony, there's a world to invade, an insatiable poem to fulfill by the
production of the cereal grains and all the fruits.
—I leave that task to the earth; I flee again toward open, empty
Space.

J'ai trouvé le secret; je sais parler; si je veux, je saurai vous dire
Cela que chaque chose *veut dire.*
Je suis initié au silence; il y a l'inexhaustible cérémonie vivante, il
y a un monde à envahir, il y a un poëme insatiable à remplir par la
production des céréales et de tous les fruits.
—Je laisse cette tâche à la terre; je refuis vers l'Espace ouvert et
vide (63).

But his desired higher calling was rejected:

And in effect I looked and saw myself suddenly alone,
Detached, refused, abandoned.
Duty-less, task-less, in the middle of the crowd,
Right-less, cause-less, strength-less, entry-less.
"Don't you feel my hand on your hand?"

Et en effet je regardai et je me vis tout seul tout à coup,
Détaché, refusé, abandonné,
Sans devoir, sans tâche, dehors dans le milieu du monde.
Sans droit, sans cause, sans force, sans admission.
"Ne sens-tu point ma main sur ta main?" (64)

Now it is time for Erato to appear onstage, the elegiac Muse, Ysé
—"Oh my shipboard friend" ("O mon amie sur le navire!"; 64):

Erato! you look at me, and I read a resolution in your eyes!
I read an answer, I read a question in your eyes! An answer and a
question in your eyes!
The joyous cry rising up from all of you like gold, like fire in the
cannon's wadding!
An answer in your eyes! An answer and a question in your eyes.

Erato! tu me regardes, et je lis une résolution dans tes yeux!
Je lis une réponse, je lis une question dans tes yeux! Une réponse et
une question dans tes yeux!
Le hourra qui prend en toi de toutes parts comme de l'or, comme
du feu dans le fourrage!

Une réponse dans tes yeux! Une réponse et une question dans tes yeux (65).

So ends "Les Muses." The other four odes are equally rich in quotable passages. Two of them are especially well known:

Hail then, oh world new to my eyes, o world that is now total!
Oh whole creed of things visible and invisible, I accept you with a Catholic [and catholic] heart!
Wherever I turn my head
I see the immense octave of Creation!

Salut donc, ô monde nouveau à mes yeux, ô monde maintenant total!
O credo entier des choses visibles et invisibles, je vous accepte avec un coeur catholique!
Où que je tourne la tête
J'envisage l'immense octave de la Création! ("L'Esprit et l'eau"; 78.)

The words I use,
Are everyday words, and they're not the same!
You won't find rimes in my poems nor any magic tricks. They're your very own sayings. Not a single one of them can't I use.
These flowers are your flowers and you say you don't recognize them.
And these feet are your feet, but watch me walk on the sea and tread the waters of the sea in triumph!

Les mots que j'emploie,
Ce sont les mots de tous les jours, et ce ne sont pas les mêmes!
Vous ne trouverez point de rimes dans mes vers ni aucun sortilège. Ce sont vos phrases mêmes. Pas aucune de vos phrases que je ne sache reprendre!
Ces fleurs sont vos fleurs et vous dites que vous ne les reconnaissez pas.
Et ces pieds sont vos pieds, mais voici que je marche sur la mer et que je foule les eaux de la mer en triomphe! ("La Muse qui est la Grâce"; 117.)

The last four odes are "L'Esprit et l'eau" ("Water and the spirit"), "Magnificat" ("My soul doth magnify the Lord"), "La Muse qui est la grâce" ("The Muse who is grace"), "La Maison fermée" ("The locked house"). They redound with themes, as one might suspect. Claudel was halfway through man's proverbial age. It was the period of his great love, the time of his rewarding marriage. As *Le Soulier de satin* was to be a score of years later, *Cinq Grandes Odes* was a sort of summa for Claudel: "My wish is to be the assembler of God's earth!" ("Mon désir est d'être le rassembleur de la terre de Dieu!"; "La Maison fermée," 138). The rest of this presentation stresses only the *Partage* theme or combination of themes.

"L'Esprit et l'eau" shows the poet greatly uplifted by God's grace, symbolized by water. Still, the mysterious Erato is sensed. The prime catalyst of "Magnificat," the name of a marial canticle, is the birth of his first child Marie (January 20, 1907). The natural importance of the Virgin Mary to Claudel, combined with this additional manifestation of creation, raised up his heart in an epiphanal song that almost thoroughly shut out thoughts of Erato. In "La Muse qui est la grâce" there is an expectable waning of the (perhaps over-) enthusiasm of the preceding ode, especially because the poet finds mystical demands of grace on him too great. Through a series of strophes and antistrophes, the Muse and the poet argue out his future. At stake even is his poetry, too terrestial and material an entity for "The Muse who is grace." His shipboard companion is, in this respect, a symbol of his vocation as a poet. The finale, "La Maison fermée," shows that the fourth ode's chidings were excessive in the direction of spirituality. For one thing, the non-mysticity of the poet's particular calling had not been taken into account. For another, it had been a question of eliminating the poet's last impurities, which had exaggerated themselves in their death throes. His friend's Beatrice role is established once and for all, and his godly or sacral role as a poet is to sing of all existence under God.

Cinq Grandes Odes is one of Claudel's great works. Aesthetically, it ranks with *L'Annonce faite à Marie* and *Le Soulier de satin*. As a record of his development as a thinker and a poet, it is on a par with *Art poétique*. And as "autobiography," it parallels the story told in *Partage de midi*. Joyous and sure exuberance characterizes the best of Claudel, because it inspires into outward expression his most hidden thoughts and feelings.[6]

Processional pour saluer le siècle nouveau (*Processional to greet the new century*) is habitually appended to *Cinq Grandes Odes*. The title and the time of composition of this long short work—it is half the length of one of the odes—make its general aim evident. Of course, the aim has already been met in "Magnificat" and "La Maison fermée," and with a natural ebullience more pleasing than the doctrinal air, not to speak of the rimed couplets, of *Processionnal*:

> Behold the outside world where lies our laic duty,
> Without scorn of one's fellow man, with love of one's fellow man,
> if I can, without violence and iniquitous passion,
> Observing the Ten Commandments better than one sees I knew how to,
> Saying my prayers morning and night and giving each person his due.

> Voici le monde extérieur où est notre devoir laïc,
> Sans le mépris du prochain, avec amour du prochain, si je le puis,
> sans violence et passion inique,
> Observant les Dix Commandements mieux qu'on voit que je ne le sus,
> Faisant ma prière matin et soir et rendant à chacun ce qui lui est dû (157).

V *LA CANTATE A TROIS VOIX*
(*CANTATA FOR THREE VOICES*)

This 1911-1912 work is even more like a play than *Cinq Grandes Odes*. Its fifty-odd pages are a dialogue between three young women—Laeta, Fausta, Beata—from sunset to dawn on the shortest night of the year, the summer solstice. The trio overlook the Rhône river, at Hostel en Valromey. Sometimes their voices alternate in a genuine dialogue, at others one of the "singers" breaks off into a song (cantique), of which there are ten. The Italian Laeta is engaged to be married on the morrow. Fausta, Polish and hence countryless (Lumîr of *Le Pain dur*!), is married but her husband is away. The Egyptian Beata was widowed after a very brief marriage. The central theme is the connection between terrestial moment and heavenly eternity, and is armatured on the relationship between men and women, that is, on love and the rose:

> Ah, I tell you, it's not the rose! it's the odor
> Breathed for a second that's eternal!
> Not the rose's perfume! it's that of the whole Thing that God made in His summer!

> Ah, je vous le dis, ce n'est point la rose! c'est son odeur
> Une seconde respirée qui est éternelle!

Non le parfum de la rose! c'est celui de toute la Chose que Dieu a faite en son été! (Beata in "Cantique de la rose," 178.)

Laeta's love is one of promise, one of Hope, Fausta's of Faith. In earthly terms, the widow Beata's is or can be the only perfect love, that which is based on Charity. Under another optic, the poem is one of absence (the widow Beata), presence (the spouse Fausta), and the link between the two concepts (the fiancée Laeta). The poem resolves the same anxieties resolved already by *Partage de midi* and *Cinq Grandes Odes*, but more tellingly because more calmly: Claudel's heart and mind have evolved and/or The searing event is fading into the past. The poem might not stand alone on the central theme of momentary love leading to eternal love were it not for the constant lyrical transfusion afforded by the ten *cantiques*, which all stay generally on course but while so doing say so much else too. For example, "Le Cantique des chars errants" ("The song of wandering carts"; Laeta) is a magnificent expansion on great clouds wandering over the Rhône valley at night. Summer, epiphany, is about to be. The night of June 21-22 ideally images this suspension before a time of magnificats. But, most profoundly, night is the mystery whereby earthly love, with its sinful contingencies, is a part of the highest love. Night leading to day, night where the gold is fabricated. Fausta the spouse and Polish exile sings this "Cantique de l'or"— "The song of gold." She says she will tell her spouse on his return that

"All that was night in me has become like gold.
All these great holdings are mine and nothing of what I acquired in your absence has lasted, but all has changed and ripened in my hands, and I see it turning into gold!"
And soon will come the day for the woman who has risen to God, clothed in a great harvest, the harvest streaming from her shoulders,
And in the moment she passes from her Spouse to her Father
What was like gold becomes like snow!

"Tout ce qui était de la nuit en moi est devenu comme de l'or.
Tous ces grands biens sont à moi et rien n'a duré de ce que j'ai acquis en ton absence, mais tout a changé et mûri entre mes mains, et je le vois qui devient de l'or!"
Et voici le jour bientôt de la femme qui est montée vers Dieu, revêtue d'une grande moisson, la moisson qui ruisselle de ses épaules,
Et dans le moment qu'elle passe à son Epoux et à son Père
Ce qui était comme de l'or devient comme de la neige! (207)

In *La Cantate à trois voix* Claudel's night theme certainly finds its finest expression.

VI *CORONA BENIGNITATIS ANNI DEI*
(CROWN OF THE INDULGENCE OF THE YEAR OF GOD)

This is in some ways an after-the-fact collage, containing pieces written as far apart as 1887 and 1914. The title, both for its meaning and for being in Latin, implies the work is another magnificat. The day, month, season, year, and the spiritual and material manifestations thereof: all are jewels in the crown of praise, love, gratitude returned to God from earth.

The fifty-six poems are divided into five sections: "La Première partie de l'année" ("The first part of the year"), "Le Groupe des Apôtres" ("The group of the Apostles"), "Images et signets entre les feuilles" ("Holy pictures and bookmarks between the [missal] pages"), "Le Chemin de la Croix" ("The Way of the Cross"). The Apostles support the crown, the Stations of the Cross mark the route. One can see the connections between *Corona* and *Processional.* Perhaps because the latter's completion at about the same time as that of *Cinq Grandes Odes* is its prime reason for inclusion with that work rather than with *Corona.* On the most immediate level, the year in question is the secular, not the liturgical, year, but this qualification is unimportant in the light of the ultimate period concerned, all earthly time. "La Première Partie" starts with "Prière pour le dimanche matin" ("Prayer for Sunday mornings"), and what is meant is the first Sunday mornings of all Januaries. "La Deuxième Partie" concludes with "Mémento pour samedi soir," that is, the last Saturday evening of the year, between Christmas and the Feast of the Circumcision. While the two sections are ordered on the regular calendar, their poems are most often inspired by the liturgy, especially the Christmas services.

Putting under one roof so many ways to look at time—secular year, liturgical year, regular week, day and night—is of course Claudelian. Another way of looking at time is provided by "Images et signets"; the title refers to the memorial or sentimental markers and religious cards a Catholic puts in his missal. Its eleven titles include an 1887 Verlaine-style piece ("Le Sombre Mai"), two searing products of the *Partage* period ("Ténèbres," "Obsession"), a homage to "Charles-Louis Philippe" (1909). Six of the poems, "Strasbourg," "Sainte Odile," the four "Images saintes de Bohème," may be here only by virtue of having met the 1915 publication deadline. The first three of all those cited are the most interesting of the hodge podge, "Le Sombre Mai" for historical reasons, the other two because of their merit.

Much of *Corona* is less accessible to those who do not know their Roman Catholic Church history and ceremony, or the Bible. In the Apostle group, while St. Peter is virtually a legend, many non-Catholics and even Catholics will not grasp all the references in "Saint Barthélemy," "Saint Philippe." But in "Saint Jude," who, a subtitle and the body of the poem both inform us, is the patron saint of desperate causes, the reader has a sufficient springboard for a finely imaged and delightful poem.

His day begins only in the evening, he doesn't start working until the eleventh hour.
He is more final than despair and cures only those who die.
It's Jude who by a single hair saves and pulls up to Heaven
The man of letters, the murderer, the whore.
He's the doctor, half-butcher, who splits open with a knife
The sinner with the Devil in his flesh but whose body must be saved with his soul.

Sa journée ne commence qu'au soir, il n'embauche qu'à l'onzième heure.
Il est plus final que le désespoir et ne guérit que ceux qui meurent.
C'est Jude par un seul cheveu qui sauve et qui tire au ciel
L'homme de lettres, l'assassin et la fille de bordel.
Il est le médecin à moitié boucher qui fend comme avec un couteau
Le pécheur qui a le diable au corps et dont on n'aura l'âme qu'avec la peau (281-82).

Such riming couplets are the most usual form in *Corona*, another reason for associating it with *Processionnal*. *La Cantate à trois voix* and *Cinq Grandes Odes* are in fact the only "volumes" of Claudel's poetry comprised exclusively, or almost, of the *verset claudélien* as it is understood in referring to his plays. It would require too much space to begin to give an idea of the individual merits of parts of the some threescore theme-rich poems. Nevertheless, perhaps only about ten of them are free enough of an immediate cult label, a label that might put off the average sophisticated reader; even the fervent believer may prefer to word his own prayers.[7]

116 PAUL CLAUDEL

VII LA MESSE LA-BAS (THE MASS DOWN UNDER)

This is a series of rimed couplet poems developed from the parts of the Mass. It was written while Claudel was in Brazil (1917-1918). There is one exception, the 1914 "Offrande du temps" ("Time's offering"), composed in Hamburg. Some of the concluding reservations about *Corona* apply here too, though not to the same extent, since *La Messe* is one third the other work's length. References to the war are frequent, not always to Claudel's glory:

> This life of sixty minutes was too long and too boring!
> For us that great Cooperative, war, to destroy all else save God!
>
> Cette vie de soixante minutes, c'était trop long et trop ennuyeux!
> A nous cette grande Coopérative, la guerre, pour détruire toute autre chose que Dieu! ("Introit," 12.)

La Messe is also concerned with the poet's exile. He had left his family behind: Back in France his wife gave birth to their daughter Renée. And he had only a few good friends to keep him company. This small nucleus was isolated by language, by war, by the general snobbishness of Rio de Janeiro's high society and diplomatic corps toward an unconventional plenipotentiary who cared little what they thought.[8] "Offertoire" provides an inkling of Claudel's feeling of isolation:

> . . . There's . . . a man who has never been able to defend himself against the sea!
> There's a man who is by profession outside everything and his domicile is to be not at home.
> No task is properly his own, he's everywhere the eternal Amateur, Guest, Dangerous Gentleman:
> Only exile teaches him his country.
>
> . . . Il y a . . . un homme qui n'a jamais su se défendre contre la mer!
> Il y a un homme qui est professionnellement hors de tout et son domicile est de n'être pas chez lui.
> Nulle tâche n'est en propre la sienne, c'est lui éternellement l'Amateur, et l'Invité partout, et le Monsieur précaire:
> L'exil seul lui enseigne la patrie (30).

This is indeed the collection's best poem. Also of key interest is "Consécration," devoted to Rimbaud. It was he who taught Claudel how to make a means rather than an end of matter, a process that has its parallels with transubstantiation. The poem also explains very well Claudel's beginnings, especially Rimbaud's role in them. "Communion" still shows the poet unable to forget Ysé, even if he has been able to resolve the problem of the rose:

Friend of my days of guilt, farewell! I renounce your thorn.
No longer do I find the rose hidden in the divine breath!

Amie de mes jours coupables, adieu! je renonce à ton épine,
Je ne retrouve plus la rose au milieu de la respiration divine! (46)

All in all, the reader who may be discouraged by some of the content of *Corona* will be less so by that of *La Messe,* title notwithstanding. "L'Offrande du temps" is outstanding for the enthusiasm that characterizes a good deal of Claudel's work. It seems to say that God's reign *has arrived.* Time's "offering" is that it has disappeared in the face of a glowing eternity:

All has become *religion,* all is bound up together,
All is glory to God in the highest and peace among men on earth.
Time is no longer, only God, and the sun has stopped,
As it was by that Jesus of old we call Joshua.

Tout est devenu *religion,* tout est ensemble solidaire.
Tout est gloire à Dieu dans la Ciel et paix entre les hommes sur la terre.
Il n'y a plus de temps, mais Dieu seul, et le soleil est arrêté,
Comme par ce Jésus jadis que nous appelons Josué (61).

And this strongly epiphanal work is not at all quietistic: "But good souls speaking of altruism, go to it! behold our fellow man...." ("Mais bonnes âmes qui parlez d'altruisme, allez-y! voici notre frère humain..."[57].)

VIII *FEUILLES DE SAINTS (PAGES OF SAINTS)*

These twenty-nine poems, composed between 1910 and 1925, comprise still less of a convincing collage than *Corona.* They are far from being his only poems of the period. Principally, there were many war poems, the first three of which appeared in 1915 as *Trois Poèmes de guerre.* The *OEuvres complètes* gather all war-poem collections under *Poèmes de guerre,* which will be discussed after this section. There are so many important or good poems in *Feuilles de saints* that they defy sufficient treatment here. The title is somewhat misleading, since less than half are devoted to "accredited" saints. Here are some remarks on the most outstanding poems, in their collection order.

118 PAUL CLAUDEL

"Verlaine" (published 1919) is of historical importance, especially since that writer, like Claudel, owes an inspirational debt to Rimbaud: Verlaine's best collection, *Romances sans paroles,* echoes the work of his youthful mentor in form and content. It is natural that Claudel should associate himself with Verlaine for this, and for the latter's Symbolist position on poetry as presented in his own "Art poétique." As we might expect, Verlaine is sympathized with and whitewashed by Claudel. For Verlaine's sake alone the poem is intriguing through its interpretation of the bohemian's miserable life. "Money, one has only too much of it for Their Honors the Professors,/Who'll teach courses on him later and who all are members of the Legion of Honor." ("L'argent, on n'en a pas de trop pour Messieurs les Professeurs,/Qui plus tard feront des cours sur lui et qui sont tous décorés de la Légion d'honneur" [68-69].)

"Ballade" (1917), one of Claudel's best poems:

The merchants of Tyre and those who do their business nowadays on the water in great mechanical imaginations.

Those whom the handkerchief still follows through that gull's wings when the arm still waving it has disappeared,

Those whose grape-arbor and field no longer sufficed, but His Nibs had his special idea about America,

Those who've left forever and who won't get there either,

All those devourers of distance, the sea itself is now being served up to them, do you think they'll get enough of it?

Once you've put your lips to it you don't lay down the cup so easily:

It'll take a long time to enjoy it, but you can try all the same.

The first swallow is the hardest.

Les négotiateurs de Tyr et ceux-là qui vont à leurs affaires aujourd-hui sur l'eau dans de grandes imaginations mécaniques,

Ceux que le mouchoir par les ailes de cette mouette encore accompagne quand le bras qui l'agitait a disparu,

Ceux à qui leur vigne et leur champ ne suffisaient pas, mais Monseur avait son idée personnelle sur l'Amérique,

Ceux qui sont partis pour toujours et qui n'arriveront pas non plus,

Tous ces dévoreurs de la distance, c'est la mer elle-même à présent qu'on leur sert, penses-tu qu'ils en auront assez?

Qui une fois y a mis les lèvres ne lâche point facilement la coupe:

Ce sera long d'en venir à bout, mais on peut tout de même essayer.

Il n'y a que la première gorgée qui coûte (73).

The refrain (italicized) plays on the saying "Ce n'est que le premier pas qui coûte," "Beginning is the hard part." Claudel wrote this near-*ballade*—except for the syllable count and the slightly relaxed rime scheme the form is authentic—on the high seas, while his ship zigzagged across the Atlantic on the way to Brazil. The combination of death wish and death fear with his basic water symbol is fortunate but not fortuitous.

"Sainte Cécile" (published 1915) is of course a pertinent poem because of Claudel's deep involvement with music. As for "Sainte Colette," her role in the formation of Violaine has already been mentioned. This poem, written in 1920 for a biography of the saint by his wife's sister-in-law,[9] may someday be instrumental in *firmly* establishing the connection between the real-life Colette and the mythical Violaine. The lengthy "Architecte" (1918) is a good introduction to the themes of architecture and/or engineering in the whole work. "Sainte Geneviève" (1918; she is the patron saint of Paris), important for its presentation of the family and woman themes, is also a sort of guide to French culture, as is another poem further on in the collection, "Saint Louis—roi de France" (1918). But it is also a war poem, whose biased nature saps its universality. The twelve short "Poèmes au verso de 'Sainte Geneviève'" (1922; "Poems written on the back of 'Sainte Geneviève'") are masterpieces of brevity; each pounds in a certain point. The subtitle is "La Muraille intérieure de Tokyô" ("Tokyo's inside wall") and walls indeed are these poems' focal points, or routes, in a godly circumscribed and delineated universe. The wall is one of Claudel's main images to express the divine purpose in all things. If part of "Sainte Geneviève" belongs in *Poèmes de guerre*, so does much of "Saint Martin" (1919):

People who can't speak and whose only outlet for self-expression is music!
Effort of blind will and physical avidity!
Nation discontent with limits and all outside forms that really apply to you,
Germany, great mixed-up pile of European tripes and guts!

Peuple qui ne sais pas parler et qui n'as issue de t'exprimer que la musique!
Effort de la volonté aveugle et de l'avidité physique!

Nation dans la mécontentement de la limite et de toute forme par le dehors qui te soit propre,
Allemagne, grand tas confus de tripes et d'entrailles d l'Europe! (160)

One can well expect to be very important the "Ode jubilaire pour le six-centième anniversaire de la mort de Dante" (1921; "Ode of jubilation for the Dante sexcentenary"). The Beatrice theme, Dante's own exile from the beloved fatherland of Florence, his desire to unify the Peninsula under Rome, his greatness. These and many other attractions made Claudel, always one for identifying with the individual studied, compare himself with Dante from one end to the other of the poem. This poem, its commentary "Introduction à un poème sur Dante" (see note 1), and *Le Repos du septième jour* (in which play the Emperor descends into Hell) all provide excellent insights into both great poets.

IX *POEMES DE GUERRE*

This classification includes four previous collections, *Trois Poèmes de guerre, Poèmes de guerre, Ainsi donc encore une fois* (*So once more*), *Poèmes et paroles durant la guerre de trente ans* (*Poems and words during the thirty years' war*). The first of these was published in 1915, the last in 1945. As has already been said, poems in other collections belong to it. A further example is to be found in *Poésies diverses* (1925-1950), "Saint Michel Archange patron des parachutistes du Corps Expéditionnaire d'Indochine" (1948). At the same time, a few of the poems are salvageable, though certainly not: "Tant que vous voudrez, mon général!" (1915; "As long as you wish, General!"), "Aux martyrs espagnols" (1937; "To the Spanish martyrs"), the poem to Pétain ("Paroles au maréchal," 1940), or the one of four years later to de Gaulle ("Au général de Gaulle," 1944). Which is neither to defend Claudel's bellicosity and politics of those times, nor to explain them. More about such matters in the conclusion; his positions were naturally identical in all of his genres. At the same time, most of the poems in the collection are undeserving of much commentary in a chapter devoted in the main to real poetry.

It is paradoxical that his most anthologized poem, one of his several very good ones, "La Vierge à midi" (1915; "The Virgin

Mary at noon"), appears in this group. It has a few references to the war, but to the uninitiated they could be about something else. Some non-coreligionists of Claudel's might have to take a giant mental step and substitute a multi-armed Hindu goddess for the cynosure in question, but perhaps not; the poem, beginning is strikingly simple:

> It's noon, I see the open church. I must go in.
> Mother of Jesus Christ, I'm not here to pray.
> I've nothing to offer, nothing to ask.
> I come only, Mother, to look at you.
> To look at you, to weep with happiness, to know it,
> That I'm your son and you're there.

> Il est midi. Je vois l'église ouverte. Il faut entrer.
> Mère de Jésus-Christ, je ne viens pas prier.
> Je n'ai rien à offrir et rien à demander.
> Je viens seulement, Mère, pour vous regarder.
> Vous regarder, pleurer de bonheur, savoir cela
> Que je suis votre fils et que vous êtes là (204).

Sacrally, the poem captures a quietistic *état d'âme*, or, profanely, a tranquil one. One could say that its frequent presence in anthologies attests to the success of this blending of the two basic senses of the word catholic. Two other poems notably do not belong in this group, except for the fact that they were written in wartime or near-wartime. "Saint Antoine de Padoue" (1916) has a delightful development somewhat akin to that of *Corona's* "Saint Jude": It is a question of lost causes in the one, lost objects in the other. "Personnalité de la France" (1938) should be more anthologized, not for its beauty but for its cultural lode and for its interest as a conceit and as being untypically Claudelian in form. Here is the first of its twelve stanzas:

> France is a star!
> France is a person,
> The hexagonal ray
> Of a star with reason.

> La France, c'est une étoile!
> La France est une personne,
> Le rayon hexagonal
> D'une étoile qui raisonne (247).

X *VISAGES RADIEUX*

The composition dates of the forty-four poems of *Visages radieux* range from 1927 to 1944. Like *Feuilles de saints*, the collection is somewhat heteroclitic. But *Feuilles* is a far better and far more interesting collection. *Radiant faces*—immediately one thinks epiphanally, and there are many passages in such a vein. "Sainte Claire" (publ. 1947):

> Take away that light which to destroy my eyes begins by doing without my ears!
> And that edible light, when you tell me it's wheat,
> I don't ask better than to believe you, but I can't do a thing about it if I don't find it appetizing.

> Otez-moi cette lumière qui pour me crever les yeux commence par se passer de mes oreilles!
> Et cette lumière mangeable, quand vous me dites que c'est du froment,
> Je ne demande pas mieux que vous croire, mais je n'y peux rien si je ne trouve pas cela appétissant (297).

"La Vision de la Chandeleur" (1945; "Vision at Candlemas"):

> And when they [those in an imagined procession] become silent, although I don't hear, there's that explosion for an answer as if of the whole firmament!
> That song you aren't allowed to hear on Earth except with your mind's ears.

> Et lorsqu'ils se taisent, bien que je n'entende pas, il y a cette explosion pour répondre comme de toutes les étoiles du ciel!
> Ce chant qu'il n'est permis sur la terre d'entendre qu'avec l'ouïe intellectuelle (308).

"Saint Jean Bosco" (1938):

> We've started believing in God again, started up again in church that Someone stronger than ourselves.
> Again we've found how to swear something to life and death.
> Just because you're old is no reason to stop being children,
> Children, men, women, we're all of us all of a piece.

> On a recommencé de croire en Dieu, on a recommencé à l'église ce Quelqu'un qui est le plus fort.
> On a retrouvé de jurer quelque chose à la vie et à la mort.

Parce qu'on est vieux, ce n'est pas une raison pour qu'on cesse
d'être des enfants,
Les enfants, les hommes, les femmes, tout cela tient d'un seul
tenant (327).

The light ("Claire") is ultimately accepted, infiltrates thoroughly into him ("Chandeleur"), then into everyone ("Jean
Bosco"). Optimism and total belief are now the largest signs on
the route whose beginnings in the 1880's are posted with suicide,
atheism and/or agnosticism, slough of despond. Getting older—
he was seventy-six in 1944—Claudel was better able to cast away
the immediate and see what he believed to be God's will on
Earth. But it is not as easy as that. A standard Christian *should*
be able to do as he. It is probably true that fear of the unknown
compensates somewhat for detachment from the material, and
this even in the believer who has no conscious reason to doubt
his own belief. The difference with Claudel was that fearless
belief had encroached upon his total being. If one studied exhaustively the death theme in his work, no doubt one would find
there was indeed an element of fear even toward the end, though
relatively minimal.

Another centralizing factor of *Visages radieux* is the predominance of poems based on saints. Predictably, they develop as do
the already cited from "Sainte Claire" and "Saint Jean-Bosco"
(patron of poor children), and as do similar poems in other collections. Still another factor is night, here both autobiographical
and thematic, that two titles, "Insomnie I" and "Insomnie II," specifically pinpoint. Others are "Dans la nuit," "Le Visiteur noc-
turne" (all four publ. 1947). There are a few earlier ones, but
those mentioned are very late and one can infer from them that
the septuagenarian Claudel had a hard time getting to sleep.

Here are additional poems of interest, in their collection order.
"La Vocation de saint Louis" (1942) is another useful cultural
poem. "Le 25 décembre 1886" (1942) is a very late reconstitution
of the most dramatic moment in his life and merits comparison
with his other descriptions of the event. This one casts aside
details and goes after the essentials. "Du côté de la défense"
(1927; "On the side of the defense") is an ironic title, because the
defendant is the nineteenth century that almost executed the
plaintiff. "Sainte Jeanne d'Arc" (1926-1945) can be usefully compared to the 1934 oratorio. And in it one finds: "I look at Joan

of Arc fallen prey to the University" ("Je regarde Jeanne d'Arc en proie à l'Université" [366]). The poem thus works out a parallel between scholastic opposition to Claudel and Joan's inability to capture Paris.

The characteristic form is the same as much that preceded and that was to follow, the rimed couplet with alexandrine-like lines, but longer and unequal. One, however, "L'Invitation à dormir" (1932; "Invitation to sleep"), *is* in alexandrines. Many seem to be conceits, or at least are untypical. "Coeur perdu" (publ. 1947; "Lost heart"): "Lost heart,/Where are you?/I'm calling it!/It bleats./ It's Milady/My poor soul!/Poor sister!/She's crying!/Do you love me?/Yes Jesus!/Oh lamb!/*Pax tibi!*" ("Coeur perdu,/Où es-tu?/ Je l'appelle!/Elle bêle./C'est Madame/Ma pauvre âme!/Pauvre soeur!/Elle pleure!/M'aimes-tu?/Oui Jésus!/O brebis!/*Pax tibi!*"; 386). There are scattered examples of greatness in this collection but one must describe *Visages radieux* as more interesting than great.

XI *POESIES DIVERSES*

This is the catchall for forty-nine of Claudel's poems written between 1925 and 1950. Because the *OEuvres complètes* volume (II) in which they appear went to press in 1952, no doubt there will be others added to this sort of collection—those Claudel wrote between this date and his death, those prior to 1952 that were omitted accidentally or on purpose. Here are cited only two, "Paul Petit" (1945) and "Le Fleuve" (1943). Petit was a dear friend of Claudel's who was shot for his resistance to Pétain and the Nazis. The beginning and end of the poem enlarge on his underground activities and his death. The middle section explains Claudel's position under the Occupation. This poem, along with "Paroles au maréchal" and "Au général de Gaulle" of *Poèmes de guerre*, must be read together. "Le Fleuve" is a chef-d'oeuvre not included in previous collections because it had served as frontispiece to Claudel's prose anthology *Pages de prose* (Paris: Gallimard, 1943); it begins:

To explain the river with water nothing, nothing else but the immense irresistible slope!
And nothing else for map and for idea than right away! and that on-the-spot devouring of the immediate and the possible!
No other program than the horizon and the sea prodigiously yonder!

Pour expliquer le fleuve avec l'eau autre chose, pas autre chose que l'immense pente irrésistible!

Et pas autre chose pour carte et pour idée que tout de suite! et cette dévoration sur-le-champ de l'immédiat et du possible!

Pas d'autre programme que l'horizon et la mer prodigieusement là-bas! (439)

Frequently in off-rimes, the poem is in the loose couplets Claudel most affected after *Cantate à trois voix*. It and "L'Esprit et l'eau" (*Cinq Grandes Odes*) are Claudel's best poetic expressions of the water-as-grace theme.

TRANSLATIONS AND PASTICHES

Poèmes de Coventry Patmore (1905-1911); *Cent Phrases pour éventails* (1925); *Petits Poèmes d'après le chinois* (1935); *Autres Poèmes d'après le chinois* (publ. 1938-1952); *Dodoitzu* (publ. 1945); *Psaumes* (1918-1955).[10]

XII   *The Oriental Influence*

All of the preceding except *Psaumes* and *Cent Phrases pour éventails* (*A hundred sentences for fans*) are straight translations. What have been called conceits in the other collections are short-lined short poems. These no doubt echo similar attempts by such as Hugo, Verlaine, Rimbaud, but Claudel's four long immersions in the Orient were also very influential, as witness his translations of Chinese and Japanese poems, plus most significantly *Cent Phrases pour éventails*, which succeed—or so it seems—in capturing the spirit of the Japanese haiku, which is composed of three lines of, respectively, five, seven, five syllables. Not that he attempts a syllabic count, or three lines; rather, he transposes these features by brevity, and by his own placing. Three other cardinal features: the leading words of the text form a column of their own, to the left; to their left are their equivalents in Japanese kanji; the French text is in Claudel's own hand. In a way, he outdid Mallarmé's *Un Coup de dés jamais n'abolira le hasard*. Here are the first three "sentences" as originally printed; for once, the English translation comes last; a lot is lost in translation:[11]

牡丹	Tu	m'appelles la Rose dit la Rose mais si tu savais mon vrai nom je m'effeuillerais aussitôt
色 句	Au cœur	de la pivoine blanche ce n'est pas une couleur mais le souvenir d'une couleur ce n'est pas une odeur mais le souvenir d'une odeur
薔薇	Glycines	Il n'y aura jamais assez de fleurs pour nous empêcher de comprendre ce solide nœud de serpents

You   call me the Rose
                         says the Rose
                       but if you knew
                       my true name
                       I would shed my petals
                         right away

At the   of the white peony
heart   there's no color
                       just the memory of a
                       color
                       there's no odor
                       but the memory of an
                       odo   r

Wistarias   There will never be
                         enough
                       flowers to pre
                       vent us from seizing that
                       solid knot of s
                         erpents

XIII *PSAUMES*

This work affords a coincidental bridge between this chapter
and the next, devoted to Claudel's prose, so much of which is
biblical. By the time of the 1966 publication, one hundred re-
workings had been located, some in several versions, not all of
them appearing in the volume. The composition dates are from
1918 to 1955. Other versions and other *psaumes* may well turn up.
More than once in his literary career, Claudel contemplated a
rendering of all one hundred fifty Psalms of David, but he never
got round to it. Are they such free renditions as to be independent poems? In his introduction Pierre Claudel says that "one
must really not see in this work a translation of the Psalms by
Paul Claudel, nor even a paraphrasing. . . . My father never tried
to translate the psalms. He couldn't imagine a more satisfactory
translation than St. Jerome's in the Vulgate" (p. 10). The book
then is not a translation, since the Vulgate is untouchable or inimitable. This is the heart of the matter. On the other hand, virtually all Claudel's *psaumes* follow the originals' verse numberings,
and the poetic liberties do not astonish. One might say they are
fairly free translations, but that Claudel did not like to call them

even that because of the awe in which he held the Vulgate. Perhaps also he did not want to harness himself into literal transpositions, for reasons related both to his personal poetic tastes and to his militant antiliteralism in things biblical.

One can understand why Claudel was so drawn to the Psalms. If he could see in himself affinities with Rimbaud, Dante, even with St. Paul, how could Claudel not identify with an apocalyptic David conversing with his God and recording his half of the dialogs under inspirational conditions and in a poetic form that were similar to Claudel's own conditions and form? Even the two ages concerned had their likenesses. Here is the beginning of his "Psaume 2" (first version):

1. Nations, what is the stirring coursing among you and when will you have stopped meditating on nothingness?
2. All the kings of the earth have risen up and all the caciques together are as one against the Lord and against the Christ [that is, the Anointed One] of Him [that is, God the Father].
3. Let us break out of their bonds, let us shake free our necks of their yoke.

1. Nations, quel est ce frémissement qui vous parcourt et quand est-ce que vous aurez fini de méditer le vide?
2. Tous les rois se sont dressés et tous les caciques ensemble ne font qu'un contre le Seigneur et contre le Christ de Lui.
3. Cassons leurs liens, secouons de notre cou leur joug! (22)

Two lexical features stand out, "cacique" (instead of "prince") and "le Christ de Lui" (instead of "Son Oint" or "His Anointed"). The first helps date the genesis of the poem, since cacique is the Latin-American word for native chief deriving from the Haitian word for lord or prince. Consequently, one looks toward Claudel's 1917-1918 sojourn in Brazil, when in fact Claudel had been given the nickname of "cacique" by Audrey Parr, the wife of the Counselor to Rio de Janeiro's British Legation; Darius Milhaud and Henri Hoppenot, Claudel's two aides, had willingly joined in on this way of referring to their superior.[12] Given Claudel's tendency to envisage Christian era events as reflections of Old Testament happenings, or even as fulfillments of prophesies, this particular psalm quite possibly attracted him for the way it prefigures the subdivision of Europe after the First World War; from his point of view, this set up an additional barrier against the communal adoration of God. Thus, if the word cacique is owing to his time in Brasil, Claudel probably wrote this version of Psalm 2 around 1920. As for "le Christ de Lui," not only did Claudel in this way stress the basic meaning of Christ—anointed—but he was returning to St. Jerome, for the Vulgate reads "adversus Christum eius"!

XIV   *In Retrospect*

In general, Claudel's theater is superior poetically to his non-dramatic poetry. The poems appear even less important in terms of Claudel's entire opus when it is considered what a small fraction of it they represent. But by no means can one overlook his strictly poetic genre, which, thanks to his genius, could not help but abound in masterpieces like "Le Porc," the whole of *Cinq Grandes Odes* and *Cantate à trois voix*, "Ténèbres," "Offertoire," "Ballade," "L'Architecte," "La Vierge à midi," and "Le Fleuve."

CHAPTER 5

Prose

P RESENTING each of Claudel's forty-odd prose titles as a separate entity is a frustrating task to the extent that the value of Claudel's themes loses out in the process. Also, there is no completely satisfactory way to divide them into groups. The *OEuvres complètes* have faced the same general problem. When their "solution" as to categorizing the prose is helpful it is used here. This is not to speak of the inability to do justice to so much in so little space; far from every essay or subdivision of each title of a non-exegetic prose work can be mentioned, much less discussed. Still, any other approach tends to sap each title of some of its individual integrity. The most promising broad divisions are into non-exegetic and exegetic, though this distinction may immediately seem imperfect because of Claudel's tendency to meander within any work short or long, and because of the concomitant difficulty of classifying even single prose collections or more unified prose-works. One must beware too of the words exegesis—or by extension non-exegesis too—in a Claudelian context, because as applied to his unofficial or personal biblical commentaries its meaning is far different from that one which is concerned with Church-approved theological explanations.

Non-Exegetic

It is practical to break down Claudel's non-exegetic prose into the following categories, some of which are centered on genres and others on themes: the Far East; *connaissances;* poetry and language; city of men; circumstantial; art criticism; correspondence; autobiographical.

I   *The Far East*

L'Oiseau noir dans le soleil levant (1923-1927); *Sous le signe*

du dragon (1908-1911); *Ecrits divers* (1911-1949). Under the
subtitle of *Extrême Orient*, vols. III and IV of the *OEuvres complètes* group these three collections plus *Connaissance de l'Est*
and Claudel's oriental-style poetry. That rallying point is adopted
in this study for the first three works cited.

L'Oiseau noir dans le soleil levant (*The black bird in the rising
sun*). Its twenty-nine pieces date from the 1920's and were published in the 1927 and/or 1929 editions of the title. Some explain
the East, mostly Japan, to the West, others the reverse. There are
some prose poems—a few of them as true chefs-d'oeuvre as anything is *Connaissance de l'Est*—a haiku, a choreography for a Japanese ballet, and three dialogs. The title, explained in the introductory "La Maison du Pont-des-Faisans" (publ. 1927; "The
house on the Bridge-of-the-Pheasants"), refers to a crow from
Siberia that returns annually to the grounds of an old Japanese
castle. The explication of the East concentrates on its art forms.
Besides the ballet choreography, in two versions, "La Femme et
son ombre" (the first written 1922, the second publ. 1952;
"Woman and her shadow"), there are essays entitled "La Poésie
japonaise" (1923), "Bougakou," "Bounrakou," "Nô," "Kabouki"
(these last four publ. 1927), "Le Poète et le shamisen (1926). Of
especial interest are the three dialogs; those are the last-named
piece, "Le Poète et le vase d'encens" (publ. 1929), and "Jules ou
l'homme-aux-deux-cravates" (1926; "Jules or the man-with-two-
ties"). Claudel's numerous dialogs in themselves could be held
to constitute a subgenre. Playlike, they are as adaptable to the
stage as *Le Neveu de Rameau* or *Don Juan in Hell*. There is an
important distinction however between them and Claudel's plays.
In the latter, not all characters speak in obedience to his own
conscience of the moment; some are villains, some exorcise his
past or momentary guilts. Also, the developing action helps direct what the characters say. On the other hand, the dialogs portray Claudel's conscience-sieved thoughts accumulating, then
eventually converging on final truths and ideas. Their one-mind-
edness can be illustrated at random. Here is the beginning of
"Jules":

JULES.—I don't know why it pleased you to rig me up with the name
of Jules which has something chubbycheeked and gamey about it.
THE POET.—My dear Jules, it's because of the hollow inside you like

a dictaphone trumpet which lets me communicate easily with the silos of our interior cavity. I say *our* because all your means of existence depend on me. I leave aside material reality. But *gamey* is a term I would never have expected.

JULES.—Well, take it as my gift to you, just as you gave me that double tie of J and L, not to speak of the charming and soldierly little knot of an *es* to finish off my name.

THE POET.—*Je* (I), *Ju*, I found in the name of Jules something caressing, confidential and sporty which you should like. Jules (Julius) Caesar descended from Venus, as you know. J and L aren't really ties; rather, they're the proverbial double ear, if you please, with which you listen to me.

JULES.—What things I have to hear!

THE POET.—You listen to me so well I scarcely have to talk. Yes, I get things back from you which, were it not for your gracious collaboration, I would hardly have understood were words (III, 306-7).

One is hard-put to pin down the unifying force in this typical dialog. Perhaps it is simply artistic creation using as vehicle certain Japanese works of art and artifacts. It is also a thematic world tour, on earthly love, the universal analogy under God, architecture, inspiration, music, and countless other topics. In effect, a case could be made for calling this and other dialogs more stream-of-consciousness, that is, a technique, than an integrated whole centered on certain subjects. One is back at the analogy. All things are part of one unity. Yet it works for Claudel, as the invisible something works which makes the *verset claudélien* inimitable for the sole "ingredient"—Claudel—that would-be imitators cannot add. Humor is rampant in this piece as it is in so much of his work, for example, the absolutely untransposable plays on words "le paon peint pond" and "le pont peint pend" (323).

Implicit in what has been said so far of *L'Oiseau noir* is much that can be said of innumerable of Claudel's shorter pieces or longer collections in any genre or subgenre. The reemphasis has been, is, and will be unavoidable. One cannot put one's finger on Claudel in terms of form versus content. The same themes are everywhere, perhaps because repetition is art's anchor. All in all, this collection is one of many helpful introductions to Claudel. And it goes without saying that because of the stress on Oriental art forms it is a valuable key to the appreciation of Oriental influences in the rest of his work, especially his theater.

Of the three Far East prose works the other two have fewer saving graces in the realms of interest and aesthetic worth. *Sous le signe du dragon* (*Under the sign of the dragon*), published only in 1948, is a series of early economic and sociopolitical essays on China, especially on the customs that were in the process of disappearing when the essays were written. Occasionally Claudelian themes assert themselves, through the primarily factual contents. In the chapter entitled "La Civilisation et le gouvernement" (written during the period 1908-1911 like the rest of the work) one senses Claudel's gusto in relating how Chinese intellectuals were kept harmless throughout their lives by being encouraged to prepare for a never-ending series of examinations. In "La Religion" he branched off into Christianity. While he always liked Asia, principally because he thought its peoples and their religions were close to God in nature, he still generally looked up to the Occident for its effect on the Orient, thus being able to write as a true colonial: "And in general one can say that the Chinese Empire owes the most materially fortunate period of its history to the Europeans and the order they established after a fashion ("L'Europe en Chine"; IV, 93). More than to the *littérateur*, this study should be of interest to a Sinologist trying to understand the new through the old, as described by a European diplomat who for all his poetic sensitivity saw things as a European.

The *Ecrits divers* (*Diverse writings*) appeared for the first time in the *OEuvres complètes* and are a catchall on the unifying theme of the Orient. There are essays on Indochina, China, Japan. Some are in the social sciences, others on the arts. Again, the colonial point of view is pervasive—see especially the 1936 "Choses de Chine" ("Chinese things")—though, in a 1952 footnote to the 1921 "Mon Voyage en Indo-Chine," Claudel wrote "I re-read with melancholy this faithful picture of a country which was, it seems, unworthily exploited by France" (IV, 344). For his own poetic art and for Oriental influences on his work, "La Poésie française et l'Extrême-Orient" (1938) is very useful. Perhaps the best piece is his 1949 speech "Une Promenade à travers la littérature japonaise," best not as a direct key to his work but because of its skillful treatment of the subject matter and because it shows that, in terms of Oriental aesthetics, Claudel knew whereof he spoke and the value of what he adapted for his own work.

II CONNAISSANCES

Art poétique (1900-1904), *La Physique de l'Eucharistie* (1910), *Figures et paraboles* (1926-1936), *Quelques Planches du bestiaire spirituel* (publ. 1949), *Le Symbolisme de la Salette* (1930-1952), *Appendices* (1931-1949).

The title of the fifth volume of the *OEuvres complètes* is *Connaissances*. Given the contents, this ingenious classification might be rendered as *God's creation recognized*, for the direct end is to say that heaven and earth are one, under God. *Art poétique* has already been presented, though as prose it may put off the reader not brought up in the French educational system, which early inculcates into its charges a tolerance for dense philosophizing. *La Physique de l'Eucharistie* (*The physics of the Eucharist*) originally appeared in *Positions et propositions II*, but is found in volume V right after *Art poétique*, with whose last chapter, "Sur le développement de l'Eglise" ("On the development of the Church"), it is relatively contemporary, and whose reasonings it extends.[1]

Ingenious though the classification may be, it is difficult to generalize about most of the essays or longer works grouped under it. Some of them are strictly Church-related, such as *La Physique*. Others are anagogical beyond the point to which literature carries, such as *Le Symbolisme de la Salette*, which deals with the occurences at Lourdes. Some others might also better be classified in the other main section of this chapter because of their biblical lode: for example, "Les Quatre Animaux sages" ("The four wise animals") in *Figures et paraboles*, an essay on exegesis as its title signifies. Some are perhaps more circumstantial than literary, for instance, two of the three *Appendices* are book prefaces.

The second most important item (after *Art poétique*) also has been previously discussed, the 1933 "Légende de Prâkriti" (*Figures*), Claudel's rebuttal to evolution as conceived atheistically. One also finds in the post-"Légende" parts of *Connaissances* many direct mentions of Prâkriti. Biblical in theme, two other *Figures* essays are completely universal by dint of their legendary subjects and artistic treatment, "Mort de Judas" ("Judas' death") and "Le point de vue de Ponce Pilate" ("Pontius Pilate's point of view"; both publ. 1933). The first is rightly much anthologized and both are masterworks of irony. Judas says: "There's always been in me a sort of curiosity, scientific, psychological or what have you, and at the same time a taste for adventure and speculation" (V, 151). *Quelques Planches du bestiaire spirituel* (*Woodcuts for a spiritual bestiary*) uses as springboard, opening anagogically upon the universe, a few selected animals: "For the contemplator animals aren't only, all of them, as was revealed to St. Peter, edible in their flesh, but edible in their spirit" ("Préface"; V, 258).

III *Poetry and Language*

Positions et propositions I (1905-1927); *Positions et propositions II* (1906-1933); *Accompagnements* (1927-1948).

The essays, speeches and gathered prefaces in these three works touch on most of Claudel's themes, especially those dealing with poetry and language. There is naturally much repetition, the individual parts are uneven in length and value, but none is valueless. The first two collections have the announced goal of uniting Claudel's considerations on the areas designated.

Positions I. "Réflexions et propositions sur le vers français" and "Introduction à un poème sur Dante" have already been described. "La Catastrophe d'Igitur" (1926) briefly and incisively states Claudel's philosophico-poetic position apropos of Mallarmé (the author of "Igitur"), Baudelaire and Poe: "But the adventure of Igitur is ended and also that of the whole 19th century. We have left behind that fatal torpor, that crushing spiritual attitude in the face of matter, that fascination with quantity. We know we are made to dominate matter and not for matter to dominate us" (XV, 116). Historically too this essay is important, for it was composed as Claudel was on the brink of his new, biblical career: "Now nothing stops us from continuing, with means multiplied to the infinite, with one hand on the Book of Books and the other on the Infinite, the great symbolic investigation which was for twelve creatures the occupation of the Fathers of Faith and Art" (117). In the short "Théâtre catholique" (1914) Claudel makes a few key statements on why he thinks religiously inspired art has advantages, and in addition explains why Catholic art is also catholic; of his *Otage* he says: "If its reception was so favorable, it's because the spectators, most of whom were foreign to my religious convictions, sensed all the same the tragic force re-

136   PAUL CLAUDEL

sulting from intervention into our individual daily lives of an outside higher call" (130-31).

Positions II. An apparent, but not the only, rationale of this collection is that some of its texts are rejects from the first volume. All the same, it contains the important and already-discussed "Propositions sur la justice"; and the first (1906) of the "Deux Lettres à Arthur Fontaine" is of prime interest for its direct prose expression of some of the key ideas to be found in the coeval "Magnificat" (*Cinq Grandes Odes*). This epiphanal statement might surprise some for emanating from Claudel: "It's a joy for me to touch all those very heavy, very real things, streetcars, sewers, electricity, and the pitiless bookkeeping" (XV, 226). Here is the ode's prime motivation: "And to me ... a child will soon be given, we're expecting it toward the middle of next month. What a joy for me, may it fulfill what was lacking in its father's destiny, that which mine would have made of me without this fatal taste for vain words!" (227)

Accompagnements. The *OEuvres complètes* collection differs from the 1949 work of the same title. Several essays are relegated to other volumes, and there are two brand new sections. Of greatest note in the new form are "Homère" (publ. 1947), "Conversation sur Jean Racine" (1954), "Victor Hugo" (1935-1952), "Paul Verlaine" (1935). They are long judgments on their subjects, as well as being implicit or explicit self-analyses. Recall how Claudel saw signs of Christ's coming in a pagan China: That is how he read Homer, and the myths Racine borrowed from. The Verlaine essay's subtitle "Poète de la nature et poète chrétien" announces its contents to a Claudelian.

One of the two completely new sections purports to continue the contents of the *Positions et propositions* collections. Some of the titles would indicate this: "La Poésie française" (1927), "La Nécessité dans le vers français" (publ. 1929), "A propos du vers français" (publ. 1961), "Sur la grammaire" (1930), "Sur la réforme de l'orthographe" (1952), "L'Harmonie imitative" (1933; this is close to the English-language concept of onomatopoeia), "Idéogrammes occidentaux" (1926), "Les Mots ont une âme" (1946; "Words have souls"). The other, least interesting, section is mostly prefaces and suffers from the inherent weaknesses of the genre. At the same time, it has the speeches "Introduction à quelques oeuvres" (1919) and "Un Poète parle de lui-même" (publ. 1961; "A poet speaks of himself"), wherein much is learned of *Tête d'or, Le Pain dur,* the *nec impedias musicam* theme, the important poem "Sainte Geneviève," and his own poetic line.

IV   *City of Men*

Conversations dans le Loir-et-Cher (1925-1928).

The 1934 preface says that "there is only a single subject on the table. I'll call it that art for men to live together, with all the improvements or degradations exerted by time and circumstances" (XVI, 10). The work is unique for being his longest prose dialog (the next longest is in *Au milieu des vitraux de l'Apocalypse*) and his longest study of its thematic subject. The "antithematic drawback" of treating Claudel's long prose works by category is perhaps greatest under "City of Men." Here for instance are two among hundreds of the passages located elsewhere that cry out for quotation in the same grouping with *Conversations*:

The Promised Land for us, of course, isn't just geographical. It's moral, spiritual, intellectual territory which the Church, and in turn each Christian under his master's sign, must conquer and reconquer, to settle in, to fall back on, with his weapons in his hands (*Emmaüs* [1946-1948]; XXIII, 252).

There is in every Christian a part which henceforth is no longer national, which is removed from all contingent controls, from all human authority, from all traditions, from all social, tribal and family obligations, which is *free* in a sense superior to the most anarchic of dreams (*Sous le signe du dragon* [1908-1911]; IV, 77-78).

The work consists of four "days." One Furius has gathered the interlocutors for the "single subject on the table." If all present are aspects of Claudel—mouthing his thoughts, perhaps, and leading the conversation toward his ideas—Furius by name and self-description is most thoroughly his creator:

My father before me had the same unsociable fierce disposition. He didn't tolerate foreign countries. He had made of his family a closed circle in which one waged battle from morn to night as if they were a municipal council. No one less than myself could stand comradeship. No one suffered more than myself from high school and the big city. No one inhaled more delightfully the good anarchic air one breathed in the France of the 90's (XVI, 12-13).

The others are Flaminius, Acer, Civilis, Florence, Palmyre,
Grégoire, Saint-Maurice. Some of these names too are symbolic
enough. One can readily predict many of the positions taken in
this work on: America, intellectuals, Combes and 1906, Church
modernism, epiphany, France, Europe. These are only some of
the topics during the first day, "Jeudi".

V *Circumstantial*

Contacts et circonstances (1913-1939); *Discours et remerciements* (1946-1947).

The classification fits better the second work than the first. The
foreword of *Discours* announces: "I assemble under this title a
certain number of separate pieces which are answers to a series
of very diverse questions, of requests for my explanations on very
disparate subjects..." (XVI, 185). At the same time, many of
the *Contacts* pieces are speeches. Public addresses would still
leave one with no real subject other than the unrevealing one of
the circumstantial. To give an idea, "Discours de réception à
l'Académie Française" (1947; *Discours*) cites among many other
entities Proust, the Catholic literary renascence, music, and one
part of a sentence says of the France of his youth: "...the bourgeois and pedagogical Universe, the prison courtyard where were
held the heavy debates of the scientists, naturalists and sceptics,
Zola, Taine, Renan, Anatole France and the whole gang, had become uninhabitable" (XVIII, 465).

Contacts. "Ma Conversion" (1909) and "Mon Pays" (1937; "My
native region") are rightly much anthologized for the influence
each subject played on his life and works. "Richard Wagner"
(1926) and "Le Poison wagnérien" (1938) interestingly disinter
his youthful misery and subsequent ire in the face of a world
that was hostile to the sort of conditions necessary to his finding
himself. One reads also between the lines reluctant admiration
for the German composer. The short book preface "Le Plaidoyer
pour le corps" (1937; "The body: the case for the defense") contains the key statement already cited but here repeated: "We go
from visible things to invisible things, not always as if from the
effect to the cause, but as if from the sign to the thing signified,
and not so much along the roads of logic as along those of analogy" (XVI, 342). "La Motocyclette" (1936) is a brief piece excellently illustrative of Claudel's epiphanal change of heart; in it is

visible his relative approval of things modern. "Le Nom" (1936; "The word") shows how Claudel rekneaded Mallarméan Symbolism into a religious loaf. "La Prophétie des oiseaux" (1939; "What the birds foretold") is central to the defense of Claudel against accusations that he entertained pro-Nazi sympathies; in it he attacks the concentration camps, citing specifically their Jewish and Polish inmates.

Discours. Besides the already-cited "Discours de réception," the "Discours de clôture à la réunion des publicistes chrétiens" (1946; "Final address at the Christian journalists convention") merits special attention. His audience seemingly on his side, Claudel inveighs against Dreyfusism, Combism, Maurrassism, Church modernism, and in addition presents an epiphanal view of Catholicism's history in this century.

VI Art Criticism

L'OEil écoute (1934-1945); *Autres Textes sur l'art* (1910-1953). The first title, signifying "the eye listens," is a synesthesic reference to painting. These two collections, the second was no doubt compounded to join the previously printed *OEil* in volume XVII of the *OEuvres complètes,* also deal with the other arts. Thus "art" here means all arts save the exclusively written arts, with painting as the focus. Because of Claudel's totally analogical outlook and since art in general is one of his great themes, much of what he said on art is also in other parts of his prose, as well as in his dramatic and nondramatic poetry. Specifically: most of his deliberations on Eastern art are relegated to his Far East essays; his correspondence with Darius Milhaud (see the following sub-section) is of course rich on music.[2] An important if expectable fugue is the advantage he saw in Christian inspiration. Not that such inspiration was absolutely essential. He believed one has to be a born artist. But he thought that once born, the artist is better off with such backing. To repeat points already made: Claudel's ambassadorship to Belgium was the catalyst for his criticisms on painting; over and above the connotations of *nec impedias musicam,* musical accompaniment to the plays, the musicality of the poetry and prose, the influence of Symbolist music, he was drawn to ballet because of his own choreographies; his sister Camille played a role in his attraction to sculpture; his

140   PAUL CLAUDEL

father-in-law's profession as an architect and his fascination for
the Middle Ages help explain his preoccupation with architecture.
  L'OEil. Not art criticism, "Avril en Hollande" (1935) is more a
travelog—sensitive travelogs could indeed be a category or theme
in itself across all of Claudel's genres—introducing the reader to
the Dutch museums against the background of April, a most apt
month for appreciating the national spirit and the great national
art. The delightful essay is thoroughly worked out. It appears as a
postscript to the 1934 speech "Introduction à la peinture hollan-
daise," which achieves the broad goal of stating the general sense
of old Dutch painting, using such exemplars as Vermeer, Rem-
brandt, Hals. Originally a newspaper article, "Ossements" (1936;
"Bones") has less to do with any of the arts than with evolution;
it is to be noted that it falls in the "Prâkriti" era of Claudel's life.
Black-and-white reproductions accompany the analyses: Four of
them are Rembrandts, including *Night watch,* the Dutch painting
Claudel most admired, and two are Hals. Claudel had much to
say of Vermeer's *View of Delft,* Proust's favorite work of art.
  Autres Textes. These are nearly all very short. The two longest, "Camille Claudel" (1951) and "Le Drame et la musique"
(1930), are the most interesting, the first for its many pronouncements on art in general and more specifically on his sister's and
Rodin's. The second was written apropos of *Christophe Colomb*
but also discusses the possible musical accompaniment to Anne
Vercors' farewell (the communion scene in *Annonce*), and the
uses of cinema in plays.

VII *Correspondence*

  Paul Claudel-Francis Jammes-Gabriel Frizeau, *Correspondance 1897-1938;* Paul Claudel-André Gide, *Correspondance 1899-
1926;* Paul Claudel-André Suarès, *Correspondance 1904-1938;*
Paul Claudel-Jacques Rivière, *Correspondance 1907-1914;* Paul
Claudel-Darius Milhaud, *Correspondance 1912-1953;* Paul Clau-
del-A. M. Lugné-Poe, *Correspondance 1910-1928;* A. du Sarment,
Lettres inédites de mon parrain Paul Claudel 1925-1955.[3]
  It may be held that Claudel's correspondence cannot be compared to the famous ones of the past, when letters were often the
most important means of communication, and when sometimes
the destinee was only so nominally. However, Claudel, removed
from the French scene for much of his life, was very dependent

on the epistolary form, and he too frequently addressed more than the apparent receiver. For instance, at a time when all three correspondents were working toward the foundation of a prayer cooperative, in a letter dated 30 May 1911 Jammes wrote to Frizeau: "I enclose an admirable letter from Claudel. What an organizer!" And since Claudel could not long refrain from bringing to the fore considerations about his own life and work, his correspondence is a rich mine on such subjects. Thus, for its intrinsic literary value or for its service as a guide to the rest of his literature, Claudel's epistolary production has received much attention from publishers. Only listed above are the correspondences that have appeared in volume form. Of these just the first four—which are the most important—are treated here. With very few exceptions, Claudel's family letters are to date unprinted. There are also the several shorter correspondences that have appeared in periodicals, not to speak of those, long or short, that are still unpublished. The Société Paul Claudel continues to amass diverse letters. Since Claudel died only in 1955, presumably many items will remain out of print for several years. Quantitatively at least, Claudel is probably as much an epistolary giant as Voltaire, whose life-span was three years less than his own.

Claudel's correspondence is especially illuminating—though this is more of anecdotal than aesthetic interest—on how in practice Claudel coexisted with his fellow mortals, be they friends or acquaintances. Rarely in the letters to or from him so far in print does one find the French intimate form of address. A notable exception proves the rule. *Tutoiement* suddenly is born, just as suddenly to disappear, in his exchanges with the French producer-director Lugné-Poe. Theater people use the form more readily than most, and the briefness of its use says more than its initial adoption. Claudel was clearly not the sentimental intimate of many. Close friendships were discouraged by his frequent moves, his triple career (diplomatic, familial, literary), perhaps most of all by his own nature. He was a solitary by choice, given to communing with himself or with his God. His temper and outspokenness often resulted in disregard for gentle expression, and the abrupt rupture of a budding correspondence. There are frequent retractions, apologies, explanations, designed to pour oil on troubled waters. Back in France in 1905, on July 21 he wrote to Jammes, who had had to cancel a meeting between them:

Jammes, you're really a nasty unreliable fellow (*proprement un sale lâcheur*). It was mostly for you I'd come to the Pyrenees; this month is probably the only part of our life that we were destined to have in common, and you're going to spend nearly all of it with some family in some place called Gers! You're a Gascon, and I no longer believe in your friendship. At least, dear friend, have fun where you are.

Already at the end he felt obliged to write: "Don't get angry at the liveliness of my letter. I'd be less vexed if I liked you less...." Writing from Eaux Chaudes (literally Hot Waters) on the Feast of the Assumption (August 15), Claudel did his best to relieve the strain he had caused: "Jammes, you boil more easily than the Eaux chaudes where I'm swimming now. I wrote you... as I would have chatted, half-seriously and half-jokingly." As for the proven or potential contribution of the correspondence to Claudelian criticism, valuable passages like this one, in a May 19, 1911 letter to Jammes, are of course countless:

... there will always be two sorts of artists, the inspired ones and the manufacturers; the inspired ones do their work more or less gropingly through a sort of divination which doesn't always preserve them from error. The manufacturers and the virtuosi please the public by the mechanical sureness of their execution, which is easily understood.

Of course, Claudel considered himself one of the inspired.

The Claudel-Jammes-Frizeau letters are unique for the attunement between the three, all dedicated converts, all quite conservative. Claudel helped make Catholics of both the bearded bard from Orthez and Gabriel Frizeau, a solid Bordeaux bourgeois. Their prayer cooperative endured over twenty years. With each other, they could rejoice in their shared religion, in their family joys, and could talk over past or contemplated actions.

The Claudel-Gide correspondence is one of the genre's twentieth-century highlights in terms of literature as well as literary history. It often reads like an epistolary novel: Claudel's goal, the conversion of his ex-Protestant renegade colleague, is pitted against Gide's oxymoronic one of maintaining his vacillating equilibrium against the onslaughts of the thundering proselytizer that was Claudel. The central characters were sometimes so near, sometimes so distant, but only depending upon which way Gide wavered; armed with his steadfast faith, Claudel ran unfalteringly roughshod over Gide's sensibilities. Gide understood what his friend was about, but the reverse was not always true. And it seems that Claudel was one of the last to learn, after *Les Caves du Vatican* (*Lafacadio's adventures*), of Gide's homosexuality. When he did, the correspondence dwindled, never to be significant again. This was much to Gide's relief. Historically, the correspondence provides insights into the life and work of the two contemporary giants, and into the intellectual and literary ambience of the early 1900's—especially the first days of the *Nouvelle Revue Française* (*NRF*), with which both were connected. Necessary adjuncts to the correspondence are Gide's post-mortems in his *Journal* of their letters and encounters.

Another evangelizing failure was Claudel's attempt with the poet and playwright André Suarès, an atheist of Israelite extraction. Unlike Gide, Suarès soon firmed up his disbelief and was unapproachable in the realm of religion. One senses a real affection on Claudel's part, more even than the warmth he extended toward Jammes and Frizeau. However, Claudel's letters to another *NRF* founder, Jacques Rivière, did meet their mark on this convert-to-be. When the conversion had been achieved, the communications died out. The Claudel-Rivière correspondence, like the Claudel-Gide, is an inestimable document.

VIII *Autobiographical*

Journal (1959-1955)[4]; *Mémoires improvisés* (1951-1952).

One is of course apt to find direct or indirect autobiography in all parts of the *massif claudélien* and, contrariwise, the above two works are autobiographical perhaps more by form than by content. The *Journal,* the first volume of which was published in 1968 and the second final one in 1969, stresses rather his spiritual and literary preoccupations; there are relatively few anecdotal details. If the amount of Claudel's correspondence is comparable to Voltaire's, his *Journal* is about as long as Gide's. The year Claudel started it—1905—was a crucial one. The entries continued until his death. Here are typical though not outstanding entries (by notebook and page number). A backward look, written in 1924:

1887-1888. My hikes by La Tournelle, composing poetry and reading *Salammbô* out loud. The sunset behind Le Géyn, over the Ourq valley. There was where I conceived *Tête d'or* and where I became conscious of my vocation, the vocation of the Universe (V, 42).

Of the same year, the beginning of a long passage on his early influences:

Books which influenced my literary formation: the novels of V H [Victor Hugo]. I never liked his poetry. At 14: Goethe—a little. At 16: Flaubert, Leconte de Lisle and above all Baudelaire (V, 48).

Although now is not the time to evaluate this work, one can see it will prove of immense worth in genesis studies, in explaining sections of his work, and in the numerous, if not representative (since he did not write it with publication in mind) passages whose quality is up to his best prose.

The *Mémoires improvisés* are the collated transcriptions of forty-two radio interviews between Claudel and Jean Amrouche. Generally, the order is chronological. Investigated mainly are known and unknown corners of his life, influences, Claudel's personal interpretations of his own works. A typical chapter summary head is:

A theological drama: *Le Repos du septième jour*—Influence of the Chinese theater—The problem of evil—*Connaissance à* [*sic*] *l'Est* (second part)—The retreat at Ligugé—Decision to abandon art—Scuttle one's will—Priesthood and poetry—It's not worthwhile to be a poet—The offering refused.

Although of course the *Mémoires* are not literary, they are on a par with the *Journal* for their value and interest.

Exegetic

Au milieu des vitraux de l'Apocalypse (1928-1932); *Un Poète regarde la Croix* (1933-1935); *Les Aventures de Sophie* (1931-1936); *L'Epée et le miroir* (1935-1937); *Du sens figuré de l'Ecriture* (1937); *Présence et prophétie* (1908-1939); *Paul Claudel interroge l'APOCALYPSE* (1940-1942); *Seigneur, apprenez-vous à prier* (1942); *Le Cantique des cantiques* (1943-1945); *Le Livre de Job* (publ. 1946); *Introduction à l'APOCALYPSE* (1946); *La Rose et le rosaire* (1944-1946); *Emmaüs* (1946-1948); *L'Evangile d'Isaïe* (1948-1950); *Trois Figures saintes pour le temps actuel* (1951); *Autres Textes religieux* (1933-1953); *J'aime la Bible* (1949-1954).

It was warned in the preface that Claudel's exegetic prose can scarcely be more than cited in this study. The seventeen titles involved are grouped in eight thick volumes of the *Commentaires et exégètes* section of the *ŒEuvres complètes*. Seven of the titles are essential, if one excepts *L'Introduction à l'APOCALYPSE*—which prefigures *J'aime la Bible*—and also the short *Livre de Job*, published in the same year *Emmaüs* was begun and which perhaps should be included under this title in future editions.

Literarily, Claudel's exegetic writings have the saving grace of his Montaigne-like tendency to escape the announced subject. An anagogic meandering, for example, may well lead the reader from the Bible to a non-biblical concern. But neither their literary nor their exegetic—respectively, their analogical and anagogical—qualities can be dwelt on here. All that can be done is to present briefly Claudel's development as an exegete, apropos of the seven key works, which are: *Au milieu des vitraux de l'Apocalypse, Du sens figuré de l'Ecriture, Paul Claudel interroge l'Apocalypse, Le Cantique des cantiques, Emmaüs, L'Evangile d'Isaïe, J'aime la Bible.*

Au milieu des vitraux de l'Apocalypse (1928-1932) was the proving ground where Claudel tried out his new subgenre. It is fascinating for being such whole-cloth Claudel, although lacking in unity of style, although restricted by the two basic forms of dialogs and letters it adopts, although it hops here and there through *Revelation* in no set pattern, and although his exegetic methods are not yet completely decided on. The optimism-pessimism duality of the New Testament work no doubt furnished the prime attraction, for Claudel was able to fit it to the anathema and jubilation which alternated in his mind. The brief *Du sens figuré de l'Ecriture* (1937) settles this last point, at least intellectually, for it takes a totally antiliteralist stand; Here his method-to-be is formally laid out. *Paul Claudel interroge l'Apocalypse* (1940-1942), while not a new version of *Au milieu,* is the first extended application of the figurative, antiliteralist method to the book of the Scriptures that above all captured his attention. The foremost reason for his fancy has just been stated, but wartime certainly added to the diatribes. *Le Cantique des cantiques* (1943-1947) shows Claudel still battling against the dragon of literalism by the very fact of his showing how much else is hidden in this potentially "dangerous" book of the Bible. *Emmaüs* (1946-1948) and *L'Evangile d'Isaïe* (1948-1950) reveal that the battle is over, with the Old and New Testaments as diptychs of the same divine picture (prefigured or in actuality) of Christ reigning triumphant over His Church. If one considers *Au milieu* as a preface, *Du sens* is the introduction and *J'aime la Bible* (1953) the summary and conclusion of Claudel's essential (in both meanings) biblical career.

CHAPTER 6

Conclusion

IT IS HARD to evaluate Claudel because of his closeness. Still, in introducing him one cannot help evaluating him. This chapter begins with a summary of the critical reception of Claudel and ends by returning to the underlying current of the whole study, namely, a personal estimation of his worth.

In a June 29, 1965 interview with me Pierre Claudel said that his father's greatest goal in life was to "arriver aux vérités," to attain the truths, this for his own sake and for that of his fellow humans. In 1930 Claudel had written:

> The general idea of my life and vocation . . . is a great desire and a great movement toward divine joy and the attempt to link to it the entire world, the world of feelings, of ideas, of peoples, of landscapes, the attempt to restore the whole Universe to its role of Paradise.[1]

And in 1952: "Catholic means universal and the first article of the *Credo* is to show us a God who created heaven and earth. Heaven and earth are beautiful!"[2]

W. H. Auden's "In memory of W. B. Yeats" reads in part:

> Time that is intolerant
> Of the brave and innocent,
> And indifferent in a week
> To a beautiful physique,
>
> Worships language and forgives
> Everyone by whom it lives;
> Pardons cowardice, conceit,
> Lays it honours at their feet.
>
> Time that with this strange excuse
> Pardoned Kipling and his views,
> And will pardon Paul Claudel,
> Pardon him for writing well.[3]

147

Many have not pardoned, do not, will not pardon Kipling his nationalism or Claudel his Roman Catholicism. This refusal to pardon assumes various forms. Word has it that there was a *Canard enchaîné* editorial entitled "Why I believe in Claudel" and signed "God." Pierre Lasserre chided:

But to run through the city exclaiming "Claudel! Claudel!" as if it were a question of a prophet and with frightful looks meaning: "Believe or die," it's the way to throw confusion into minds, and also to sow aversion among those whose esteem counts.[4]

It is not so much Claudel as his aliterary cult that Lasserre attacked, but one can read a *literary* judgment between these lines by Henri Clouard:

There is one way to read Claudel's ideologies with the minimum of irritation: All you have to do to forget his fantastic syntheses and his false prophet exaltations is to translate the philosophy game into poetic and mythical reality.[5]

Clouard and Lasserre are both traditionalists, classicists. That too explains why they are not fervent Claudelians. Another possible area of attack is called "Claudel's error" by Pierre-Henri Simon. Here is his description of it:

Certainly not in adhering to a religious dogmatism which gives equilibrium to his thought and peace to his heart, thus freeing his exceptional creative power, but the melding of certitude on the level of supernatural truths, necessary for a Christian, with that of philosophical and moral opinions, in which the spirit of prejudice and the demon of self-love menace the Christian as any other son of woman.[6]

Here Claudel's philosophy is found faulty, and the cause of the attributed failing gratuitously provided. Simon's judgment is apropos of Claudel's pro-Francoism, which obviously derived from the way he took his religion. Claudel was also a Kipling; rooted primarily in chauvinism—though abetted by such as Luther and Kant—was the anti-Germanism for which many have criticized him.[7]

If literary critics claim to have their *partis pris* or set purposes, they frequently attenuate these in print for fear of later being adjudged egregiously wrong. This timorousness translates as apparent humble fairness toward what one dislikes, or so often this seems to be the case: The critic and the historian as manualists frequently play political hide-and-seek. Without such self-imposed restraints, what would all those quoted really say against Claudel? The cacaphonic "rasoir"—"razor," but used as an adjective it means "very boring"—is the word that many young French intellectuals would use to describe Claudel, and the reaction has its transposition on this side of the English Channel and the Atlantic Ocean among those intellectuals who have "got through" more than just *L'Annonce faite à Marie*. Perhaps the manual-style evaluations are not negative enough in their negativism. In the eyes of many, Claudel's claim to a permanent berth in the history of real literature is not established: And that is why, whether or not one agrees with critics like Edmund Wilson and Simone de Beauvoir, it is refreshing to read their franker judgments. The first two passages are in Mme de Beauvoir's second volume of autobiography:

> This evening I re-read *Tête-d'or*, which I find beautiful, especially Cébès' death; but it's a fascist play, and even nazi.

> [Apropos of her and Sartre's reactions to Barrault's wartime production of *Le Soulier de satin*:] Many things in the drama had gone against our grain when we had read it a few years before; all the same, we had liked how Claudel had successfully upheld, in a single love, both heaven and earth. He had disgusted us completely since he had written his "Ode au maréchal". . . .[8]

She rather liked the performance. Edmund Wilson was more exclusively aesthetic:

> Inedibility of Paul Claudel: I saw that the Barrault company was doing Claudel's play *Le Soulier de satin*. I thought that I ought to go, and got the text to read it first. Though I had never been attracted by what I knew of Claudel, I had a certain curiosity about him, and especially about this play. . . . But I only lasted half-way through, and I felt I couldn't face a performance. I have rarely disliked a book so much. There are occasional gleams of poetry, but the combination of rhetoric and religiosity, the supersexual and antisexual idealism that seems so effortful and not quite sincere, was rejected by my literary stomach. The preposterous hero and heroine are prevented from consummating their passion by the fact that the latter is married, and they are supposed to be enjoying a higher bliss through the self-denial this imposes. . . .
> Yet some passages of *Le Soulier de satin*—in which the characters do a great deal of travelling and which does aim at a certain universal scope—made me feel again the flimsiness of human life.[9]

At the same time, the unreservedly enthusiastic voices are
legion. In *Le Confort intellectuel* Marcel Aymé shows how dia-
metrically wrong was the first general reaction to Proust, who is
the soul of clarity, which termed him hermetic.[10] Just as Proust's
lengthiness was mistaken for obscurity, it may be a similar error
to allow Claudel's religiosity and chauvinism to distract too
much. Saint-John Perse and Léopold Senghor are greatly indebted to his work as a source of their own inspiration. That art
transcends politics and religion is manifest in the natural admiration in which Claudel is held by Louis Aragon. Or take Jean
Vilar, actor-producer-director; his involvement with the Left in
no way prevents him from idolizing Claudel. Not to mention
Vilar's fellow great, Jean-Louis Barrault—one can describe him as
areligious—who has done so much to propogate Claudel's theater.
Some of the manualists seem completely for him but as judges
they may be suspect for reasons just cited. Better to finish with
the testimony of Eugène Ionesco:

... when you sweep away all the ideological trash of the Nineteenth
and early Twentieth Centuries, *Ubu* [Alfred Jarry's *Ubu roi*] is one of
the few theatrical works that is left. It, and Paul Claudel's theater....[11]

I had always known Claudel was a great poet. Now, after having again
encountered him by going to see *Tête d'or* this winter at the Odéon,
in the Jean-Louis Barrault production, I realized, all of a sudden, that
Paul Claudel is certainly the greatest poet of the 20th century: not
only for highly literary qualities, an unimaginable verbal power, a
tragic grandeur one meets only, and I mean this, among the few very
great universal poets but (and perhaps above all) for his forceful
reintegration, in their exact places, of the values in the hierarchy of
the cosmic order.[12]

With Claudel dead less than two decades, his most fervent
admirers must only marvel at the editions of his work and
studies on him appearing in the French language. There is the
complete works in progress, now in its twenty-sixth volume
and already almost sold out. As of early 1970, Claudel is in six
volumes of the hallmark of French publishing, the Bibliothèque de la Pléiade. Seven plays, one poetry collection, two
prose works are already in very cheap pocketbooks. There have

been countless regular trade editions of various parts of the
massif. There exist two important *Cahiers* series—one French,
one Canadian—and a yearly volume on a Claudel theme offered
as a number of *La Revue des Lettres Modernes*. The sponsoring
house of the same name, *Les Lettres Modernes*, publishes many
Claudelian studies under the editorship of Michel J. Minard. The
leading Claudelian is the youthful Professor Jacques Petit of the
University of Besançon, whose vast production on Claudel pales
only before his total bibliography. There are Claudel societies in
Belgium, Canada, France, Germany, Greece, Japan, Lebanon,
and the United States. Of these, five have regular or occasional
publications. The Société Paul Claudel of Paris, which has connections with Claudel's descendants, also has an archive that has
overflowed into a section of the Bibliothèque Sainte Geneviève.
This society's bulletin, almost forty numbers to date, is the central one. Especially awaited, is the publication of the complete
Claudel bibliography, by Jacques Petit for *Les Lettres Modernes*.
There are still other unpublished works. There still must come:
a general correspondence; a definitive biography (there has been
nothing close to one so far); an indexed complete works (only
volume XVIII of the current *OEuvres complètes* has an "index of
writers referred to"). One cannot begin to speak of the French-
language productions of Claudel's plays. Suffice it to say that
Barrault's wartime *Soulier* opened flood gates that remain open.
It is all to Claudel's advantage and merit that France's two top
theater men (Vilar and Barrault) are enthusiastic apostles.

What of Claudel's fate outside the French language? Sardon-
ically, it can only improve. Realistically, only in translation can
his work have an impact in non-French-speaking areas. Here and
there in America and England, a Catholic institution stages *The
tidings brought to Mary*, scenes from *The satin slipper*, or an
amateur chorale attacks *Joan at the stake*. Not many read Saint-
John Perse in translation. Fewer know aught about Claudel.
Those of his works that have been rendered into English have
suffered in the process. Germany, already Shakespeare's and
Shaw's second home, has accepted Claudel in a significant manner.[13] With this exception, Claudel's situation abroad can only
improve.

There are those who skirt Barcelona because of its beggars'
mountain, those who avoid Proust because his novel is not a fin-

ished work of art, or even because of its author's personal life. Though Claudel was an artist, not a philosopher, some of his points of view put some people off, his religiosity above all. Everyone has a religion, from pope to anarchist. Critics often go back on any offer they may have made of generous neutrality toward a writer's religion. Subtlety in preaching one's cause is an attribute, but only if that subtlety's motivation is disinterestedly authentic. Claudel was too enthusiastic for his authenticity to affect pragmatic disinterest. If one can question Claudel for his obvious religiosity, may one question the motives of those who are more subtle: ego or conviction?

As for Claudel's diatribes and political positions, Kiplingesque or Claudelian, the essential is to view them in certain perspectives. First, of one's own diatribes. Second, of others' diatribes that become unconsciously one's own. After the Second World War, Pétain was inculpated, Hirohito exculpated. In terms of absolutes, or if there were absolutes, it should have been the other way round. And now Pétain is being exonerated. It is not reasonable to attack Claudel in the 1940's for his ode to Pétain, then to whitewash Pétain in 1970. A third perspective concerns Claudel's own and authentic one of creation, a predictable and essentialist perspective in regard to such as Luther and Franco. Claudel effectively abdicated his independent reasoning powers here and there in favor of a system, but the whole of literature can be examined for more subtle—thereby more deceitful?—similar abandonments. And if a Catholic or a non-Catholic objects that, as a Catholic, Claudel was not necessarily obliged to castigate the Loyalists and praise Franco's Spain, this would deny Claudel's right to act vis-à-vis of his religion in the way he chose to act. The Catholic who so criticized Claudel would by extension be severely limiting his own freedom of opinion, and such a criticism from a non-Catholic would be odd indeed, like complaining that Catholics are just as sinful as Protestants.

From another somewhat defensive angle, two terms, desacralization and poetic state of mind (*état d'âme*), are crucial to arguing against certain anti-Claudel judgments. Desacralization is an objective attempt to find common ground on which to meet, excluding theological considerations. One critic describes as "inexplicable neglect" the paucity of English translations of Claudel's works and says that one of the reasons

... relates to the special nature of Claudel's mystic angle of vision of the world. ... the whole of Claudel's poetic drama is built upon the two basic themes of love and redemption. ... In each case he brings before us two lovers who, we are to understand, have through all time been meant for each other ... and at the same time their final union must perpetually be denied, since in its very perfection it would exclude God. ... There cannot be but something repellent in this idea of a God-Fisherman who raises his creatures to him with a hook in their hearts. ...[14]

This is like levying a complaint against the philosopher who does not live his system twenty-four hours a day: Sartre should be so full of existentialist anguish as to never enjoy himself. More to the point, these ideas, desacralized, say that physical love blinds one to one's own true duties. Even if the critic were correct, that is, if Claudel effectively preached against such love (not simply warned of the dangers of love), this finds a parallel in existentialism, which says that in love either one's own or the loved one's liberty is destroyed. Many of Claudel's positions can indeed be desacralized. Subtracting the last two words from his concept of the universal analogy under God makes it revert to a Baudelairian interpretation, except that it would be something central for Claudel, while it was not so authentic a concept for Baudelaire, who used it more than he depended on it. And removing divine grace from what Claudel said of inspiration still allows many rich insights into the workings of the poetic muse. Of course, not all his thought can be so processed. His promotion of the Catholic Church can remain only that. What would he himself have thought of desacralization as applied to him? Pragmatically, he probably would have said that it could be a beginning for some of those setting out on the road that leads from the visible to the invisible. Only relevant here though is that Claudel *can* be profitably desacralized. What he said of his theater applies to more than it:

All I can say is that to get something from my plays there is precisely no need to be a Christian, all you simply need to be is, so to speak, a Claudelian; no more than, to get something from Homer, would you have to believe in the various gods, in the various supernatural powers that he sends across the stage, but you must at least have a certain sense of the supernatural, a certain sense of the moral grandeurs, of the providential grandeurs which continually enter into human affairs.[15]

A state of mind, *état d'âme*, is not philosophy. *Qua* poet, what Claudel showed the world were successive *états d'âme*. *Qua* ambassador and would-be apologist, he intended to demonstrate something more reasoned, but this did not always work out, and one finds the poet dominating in unexpected places in his work. Claudel's reasonings, when exclusively that, are not always correct. Sometimes they are infused with a poetic spirit, and have no reasonable handle to be grasped by. Sometimes what he tried to pass as reasoning was not that in any way. It was simply poetry. So a diatribe against Germans in any of his genres may have sprung from an emotional reaction to a morning wartime headline, a lashing of Luther and all Protestantism may be the depressive reflex after a manic elation toward his God.

To repeat, Claudel created quickly, did not reread or rewrite formally, altered only incidentally, while preparing a clean copy for the printer. That is *état d'âme* composition *nec plus ultra*. All the same, a "philosophy" for Claudel can be pasted together into a collage that resolves contradictions or incongruities. One has to resort to both internal and external evidence. When Claudel was alternately for and against material progress this was apocalyptic or *état d'âme*-like, psychologically true. The plottable trend away from deprecating it and toward appreciating it shows a definite and reasonable evolution. Claudel's attacks against Kant are more cant than anything else. He learned something of him in lycée, not much, and the castigation of that one individual is part of Claudel's "blockbuster" handling of the nineteenth-century ambience that almost did him in. The tactic is of course unfair personally, but Claudel was fighting fire with fire. This has to be realized, and appreciated. Which brings one, if one is not already there, to Kant's country of origin. After three Franco-German conflicts any French objectivity on the subject of Germany may seem to some a minor miracle. Claudel alternated his anti-Germanism with many conciliatory gestures. And his message of love makes it impossible to hold that he *philosophically* rained anathema on all Germany. In sum, the idea content of his work must be approached in the light of his poetic nature, the evolution of his thought, and its Frenchness and Catholicity.

One way for a writer to influence his readers is first to persuade them that he thinks as they do. That accomplished, he can then mix in some of his own values. Claudel could not cool his ardor long enough to be subtle in this way; his is generally a shock literature that could be called the hard sell. Perhaps such absolute authenticity is a pleasant encounter for many readers in this present most compromising of worlds.

Another admirable quality is Claudel's mature approach to the life situation, though this is of more philosophical than literary interest. Claudel scorned the crutches of memory and the past, was concerned only with the present and the future. Though his approach to modern times was biased, at least it was constructive, and often in a way that had affinities with existentialism. For example, the great message of *L'Annonce faite à Marie* is that of charity, of an open or rule-less—existential—morality. Late in life Claudel described in the following way the change in his "social" orientation, which took place at the beginning of the century: "In a train compartment, one seat faces forward, the other backward; some watch the past fading away, others watch the future approaching. . . . At that time I changed seats; from the one facing backward I moved to the seat facing frontward."[16]

Generally, and if one suspends one's prejudices for or against a religion-directed literature, one should find in Claudel an enthusiastic, joyous, beautifully-styled interpreter of the universe, a man endowed with an especially accurate vision of existence, and who had valuable things to say and to show to others. Since Claudel's full potential is far from realized in France, it is understandable that he has not yet been sufficiently recognized elsewhere, even in Germany, which is the foreign country most aware of Claudel. But the process toward universal recognition has begun. Among non-francophones, it necessarily is and will be a question of translations. As for Claudel in English, gone will be the inherent value of the magic original lexicon. But worthy substitutes will be found often enough, if poets are the translators. That English and French word orders are similar will be of help, especially in terms of the Claudelian iamb, so important to the Claudelian poetic line. Admirers of Shakespeare should not need much extra conditioning to like Claudel. His time will come. Until it does, it is the English language's loss.

Notes and References

Chapter One

1. I am greatly indebted to the following works for this highly eclectic biography of Claudel: Louis Chaigne, *Vie de Paul Claudel et genèse de son oeuvre* (Paris: Mame, 1962); Paul-André Lesort, *Paul Claudel par lui-même* (Paris: Seuil, 1963; "Ecrivains de Toujours #63"); Jacques Madaule, *Le Drame de Paul Claudel*, "édition entièrement mise à jour" (Paris: Desclée de Brouwer, 1964); *Cahier Paul Claudel I—TETE D'OR et les débuts littéraires* (Paris: Gallimard, 1959); Paul Claudel, *Mémoires improvisés* (Paris: Gallimard, 1954) and *J'aime la Bible* in *OEuvres complètes*, volume XXI. To date there are twenty-six volumes in the *OEuvres complètes* (Paris: Gallimard, 1950-1967), henceforth *OC* when convenient. Location in *OC* is indicated by roman numerals for volumes, arabic for pages. Unless otherwise indicated, dates provided are of composition.

2. See *"Tête d'or 1949,"* in *Paul Claudel 2—"le regard en arrière"—quelques drames et leurs versions successives*, ed. Jacques Petit (Paris: Lettres Modernes, 1965), pp. 47-71.

3. *Cahier Paul Claudel I*, p. 117. English translations are mine.

4. *Mémoires improvisés*, p. 21.

5. In his *L'ENDORMIE de Paul Claudel ou la naissance du génie* (Ottowa: Editions de l'Université d'Ottawa, 1963 [*Cahier Canadien Claudel 1*]) Eugène Roberto establishes fairly well that *L'Endormie* was written in 1886 or early 1887; see especially pp. 15-16. Henri Mondor, in his *Claudel plus intime* (Paris: Gallimard, 1960), had already expressed serious doubt about the 1882 or 1883 date Claudel had customarily ascribed to the play (pp. 37-53).

6. Jacques Rivière-Paul Claudel, *Correspondance 1907-1914* (Paris: Plon, 1926), p. 75; letter dated August 4, 1907.

7. See notably "La Catastrophe d'Igitur" (1926; *Positions et propositions I*; XV, 111-17), "Notes sur Mallarmé" (1913?; *Accompagnements*; XVIII, 125-26).

8. *Cahier Paul Claudel I*, p. 138. For the Mallarmé quotation following, see p. 41.

9. Pp. 92-94.

10. *Cahier Paul Claudel I*, pp. 60-111.

11. *Ibid.*, p. 94. The next *Cahier* has for a central theme the study of versions.

12. Some critics point out that Claudel and Huysmans were at Ligugé at the same time, but do not know if they met. They did. A 1924 entry in Claudel's *Journal* reveals that he met "Huysmans

156

two or three times in the summer of 1900 at Ligugé when I wanted to become a Benedictine" (notebook #5, p. 49).

13. On this theme in Claudel see notably: Lily Maurer, *Gestalt und Bedeutung der Frau im Werke Paul Claudels* (Zurich: Ernst Lang, 1947); Ernest Beaumont, *The theme of Beatrice in the plays of Claudel* (London: Rockliff, 1954), translated by Huguette Foster, *Le Sens de l'amour dans le théâtre de Paul Claudel* (Paris: Lettres Modernes, 1958).

Chapter Two

1. See his *Art poétique* (1900-1904), V, 35.

2. So far there are no fullblown theme studies. The two books most oriented in this direction are: Gérald Antoine, *Les CINQ GRANDES ODES de Claudel ou la poésie de la répétition* (Paris: Lettres Modernes, 1959); *Paul Claudel 3—thèmes et images,* ed. Jacques Petit (Paris: Lettres Modernes, 1966). Donat O'Donnell examines a few themes in his *Maria Cross* (New York: Oxford University Press, 1952; pp. 167-200 deal exclusively with Claudel). Some themes and subthemes are listed in: *Paul Claudel par lui-même*; Paul Claudel, *Mes Idées sur le théâtre* (Paris: Gallimard, 1966).

3. Similar compendiums could be arrived at by quoting from various parts of his work, especially the single 1925 essay "Réflexions et propositions sur le vers français" (*Positions et propositions I,* XV, 9-56), which paraphrases and/or elaborates on many points in *Art poétique*. A more ambitious after-the-fact compendium, containing this essay, is Paul Claudel, *Réflexions sur la poésie* (Paris: Gallimard, 1963).

4. His first published collection of plays was entitled *L'Arbre (The tree;* Paris: Mercure de France, 1901).

5. Three fuller treatments of the *verset* are highly recommendable: Alexandre Maurocordato, *L'Ode de Paul Claudel* (Geneva-Lille: Droz-Giard, 1955), pp. 21-38; Joseph Boly, O.S.C., *L'ANNONCE FAITE A MARIE—étude et analyse* (Paris: Editions de l'Ecole, 1957), pp. 82-95; André Lagarde, *et al, XXᵉ Siècle* (Paris: Bordas, 1962), pp. 180-82.

6. H. W. Fowler, *A dictionary of modern English usage* (London: Oxford University Press, 1952).

7. *Cahier Paul Claudel II—Le Rire de Paul Claudel* (Paris: Gallimard, 1960).

8. See André Vachon, *Le Temps et l'espace dans l'oeuvre de Paul Claudel* (Paris: Seuil, 1965).

9. *Ibid.* Vachon finds however that Claudel is more an Easter (death) than a Nativity (rebirth in this case) Christian.

10. See notes 8 and 9, this chapter.

11. On the sometimes related, sometimes identical, themes of love and woman, see works cited in note 13, chapter I.

12. See John MacCombie's doctoral dissertation, *"L'Ange et la bête*: a study of the influence of Rimbaud on Claudel"* (Yale, 1965).

13. The classification title is borrowed from my own doctoral disseration, "Claudel and the city of men" (University of Washington, 1956).

14. Claudel used the specific terms positive justice and negative justice for the first time in his 1910 essay "Propositions sur la justice" (*Positions et propositions II*, XV, 160-165).

15. On the resurgence see especially: Joseph Calvet, *Le Renouveau catholique dans la littérature contemporaine* (Paris: Lanore, 1927); Louis Chaigne, *Anthologie de la renaissance catholique* (Paris: Editions Alsatia, 1938); Adrien Dansette, *Histoire religieuse de la France contemporaine*, volume 2 (Paris: Flammarion, 1951).

Chapter Three

1. This is found in Madaule's introduction to the theater volumes of *OC* (VI, 7).

2. Henry Clouard, in his *Histoire de la littérature française du Symbolisme à nos jours*, 2 volumes (Paris: Albin Michel, 1947), is one of the few literary historians to conscientiously maintain the distinction between externals and internals. His various sections on Claudel are interesting for this reason especially. Such traditionalism is a good palliative against those who claim to admire Claudel for literary reasons when their reasons are really extraliterary.

3. *Op. cit.*

4. See note 5, chapter I.

5. Act I, or "première partie," in volume VI of *OC*, pp. 69-70; there are no scene divisions in this play. When it is convenient and/or necessary to do so, play divisions and locations in *OC* are furnished parenthetically in the text. When both types of information are provided, the divisions occur before a semicolon, the locations after it. This quotation could be indicated as: (I; VI, 69-70).

6. In his *Mémoires improvisés*, p. 69.

7. See Bernadette Bucher, "L'Arrière-plan amérindien de *L'Echange*," *La Table Ronde*, no. 194 (March 1964), pp. 112-133, or its subsequent form as "Paul Claudel et le monde amérindien," in *Claudel et l'Amérique* (Ottawa: Editions de l'Université d'Ottawa, 1964 [*Cahier Canadien Claudel 2*]), pp. 85-121.

8. See Claudel's 1900 letter to the actress Marguerite Moreno, reproduced in Pierre Champion's *Marcel Schwob et son temps* (Paris: Champion, 1927), p. 271.

9. For a more detailed comparison see Floriane Paoletti, *"Tête d'or 1889-1894,"* in *Paul Claudel 2,* pp. 25-45. Jacques Petit's introduction to the volume, *"En art il n'y a pas de définitif"* (pp. 7-24; his title is a quotation from Claudel), is an excellent summary of its general subject: Claudel's habit of writing second (and more) versions.

10. Paul Claudel-Francis Jammes-Gabriel Frizeau, *Correspondance 1897-1938* (Paris: Gallimard, 1952), p. 130.

11. See a discussion of this in Barna M. Avré, *L'OTAGE de Paul Claudel—essai de psychologie littéraire* (Québec: Le Soleil, 1961), pp. 45-50. A valuable explication of the play is Pierre Brunel, *L'OTAGE de Paul Claudel ou le théâtre de l'énigme* (Paris: Lettres Modernes, 1964).

12. In a 1948 newspaper article Claudel himself stressed the medieval associations of the placenames of the first two Violaine plays. See the notes to vol. IX of *OC,* pp. 293-94, where the article is reprinted.

13. *Mémoires improvisés,* p. 253.

14. For the relationship between the poet and the musician see *Cahier Paul Claudel III—Correspondance Paul Claudel-Darius Milhaud* (Paris: Gallimard, 1961). The preface by Henri Hoppenot (pp. 7-24), also assigned to the French ministry at Rio de Janeiro with Claudel and Milhaud, throws a refreshing light on Claudel's day-to-day existence. Jacques Petit's introduction (pp. 25-31) summarizes the relationship excellently.

15. This is what he said in a commentary to an edition of twelve lithographs by Emilienne Milani on themes from his *Cantate à trois voix* (Paris: Éditions d'art Sagile, 1946). The commentary is reprinted in *OC* (I, 401).

16. He told of this meeting in *Mémoires improvisés,* p. 269.

17. Henri Mondor, *Claudel plus intime.*

18. Madaule, *op. cit.,* is far kinder to the last two *Partage* and the second *Echange;* pp. 398-412. See again note 9 of this chapter on second versions.

Chapter Four

1. "Religion et poésie" (1927), *Positions et propositions II;* XVI, 148-49.

2. "Le Plaidoyer pour le corps" (1937), *Contacts et circonstances;* XVI, 342.

3. With one exception, through *Corona* these collections are in volume I of *OC,* the others in volume II. The exception is *Connaissance de l'Est,* in volume III. In this section only pagination for references and citations is provided.

4. The presentation for *Connaissance* draws heavily on an excellent

synthesizing article by Renée Riese Hubert, "Claudel, poète en prose," *French Review*, volume XXXV, no. 4 (February 1962), 369-76.

5. See the December 14, 1904 letter from Claudel in André Suarès-Paul Claudel, *Correspondance 1904-1938* (Paris: Gallimard, 1951), p. 27.

6. Four works are especially recommendable for an indepth study of *Cinq Grandes Odes*: Antoine and Maurocordato, *op. cit.*; H. J. W. van Hoorn, O.F.M., *Poésie et mystique* (Geneva-Paris: Droz-Minard, 1957); Marius-François Guyard, *Recherches claudéliennes autour des CINQ GRANDES ODES* (Paris: C. Klincksieck, 1963). Ernest Beaumont appraises and reviews the second and third books in his *L'Ode claudélienne—deux exégètes* (Paris: Lettres Modernes, 1958).

7. It would be malapropos in this study to assume a coreligionist attitude in discussing such poems, although this might well have satisfied the poet. One can imagine, furthermore, that this attitude can do a lot of harm to the cause of objectivity. At the same time, Madaule, *op. cit.*, is an exception. He is a most Catholic Claudelian, but in his case it helps.

8. See note 14, chapter III.

9. Elisabeth Sainte-Marie-Perrin, *Vie de Sainte Colette* (Paris: Plon, 1921).

10. The translations of the Patmore poems have not yet appeared in *OC*. They are however in Paul Claudel, *OEuvre poétique* (Paris: Gallimard, 1962; "Bibliothèque de la Pléiade"). *Psaumes* also is yet to appear in *OC*. Parts have appeared elsewhere, but the only relatively integral edition is the 1966 Desclée de Brouwer one. The other collections are in *OC*, volume IV.

11. The *OC* version lacks the kanji and the handwriting. The reproduction here is of the 1942 Gallimard edition, which in turn reproduced the original 1927 one (Tokyo, Editions Koshiba).

12. See note 14, chapter III, and the note on page 252 of *Psaumes*.

Chapter Five

1. Apparently by oversight, *La Physique* is maintained and repeated in *Positions II* (*OC*, XV).

2. See also on music Joseph Samson, *Paul Claudel poète-musicien* (Paris: Milieu de Monde, 1948).

3. Fuller and more accurate bibliographical information is provided in the bibliography proper. In the text, the date limits of the correspondences are given as if they are part of the titles, though this is not necessarily the case. The last item is of dual authorship though in this instance it is the bibliographical information that might mislead, or the title.

4. Locations in the *Journal*, which is published in two Bibliothèque de la Pléide volumes, refer to the original notebooks and their pagination.

Chapter Six

1. In "Préface à Jacques Madaule," *Accompagnements*; XVIII, 327.
2. *OC*, XXI, 486. This is part of a *J'aime la Bible* variant.
3. *British literature*, volume II ("from Blake to the present day"), eds. Hazelton Spencer, *et al* (Boston: D. C. Heath, 1952), 946.
4. Pierre Lasserre, *Les Chapelles littéraires* (Paris: Garnier, 1920), p. xii. No impassive Sebastian, Claudel returned the arrows. In *Le Soulier de satin* textbook grammar is ridiculed by its personification in Don Pedro de las Vegas, who in an earlier draft was called Don Pedro de las Serras (see *Mémoires improvisés*, p. 178).
5. Clouard, *op. cit.*, volume I, 477.
6. Pierre-Henri Simon, *Histoire de la littérature française au XXe siècle*, volume II (Paris: Armand Colin, 1957), 29.
7. See especially Margaret Andersen, *Claudel et l'Allemagne* (Ottawa: Editions de l'Université d'Ottawa, 1965 [*Cahier Canadien Claudel* 3]). By and large, German critics have been less sensitive to Claudel's anti-Germanism than non-Germans!
8. Simon de Beauvoir, *La Force de l'âge* (Paris: Gallimard, 1960), pp. 410, 578.
9. Edmund Wilson, "Notes from a European diary 1963-1964," first installment: *New Yorker*, May 21, 1966, pp. 61-62.
10. Marcel Aymé, *Le Confort intellectuel* (Paris: Flammarion, 1949), pp. 161-65. The fictive Lepage speaks for Aymé.
11. In an interview with Gabriel d'Aubarède, *Les Nouvelles Littéraires*, March 8, 1962.
12. Eugène Ionesco, "Ce que j'aurais voulu mieux dire," in *Cahier Paul Claudel II*, p. 27.
13. See note 7, this chapter. Dr. Andersen's book treats this subject exhaustively.
14. Anon., "Love and redemption," *The Times Literary Supplement*, October 15, 1954, p. 654. This is a review of Joseph Chiari, *The poetic drama of Paul Claudel* (London: Harvill Press, 1954).
15. *Mémoires improvisés*, p. 282.
16. *Ibid.*, p. 96.

Selected Bibliography

Part I: *Primary Sources*

(First publication is indicated, also, location in *OEuvres complètes* volume is given parenthetically at end of entry.)

Accompagnements. Paris: Gallimard, 1949 (XVIII).

L'Annonce faite à Marie. 1910-1911 version—Paris: Gallimard, 1912 (IX). 1948 version ("édition définitive pour la scène")—Paris: Gallimard, 1948 (IX).

Art poétique. Paris: Mercure de France, 1907 (V).

Au milieu des vitraux de l'Apocalypse. Paris: Gallimard, 1966 (XXVI).

Autres Poèmes d'après le chinois. First in *OC* (1952, IV).

Autres Textes religieux. First in *OC* (1965, XXV).

Autres Textes sur l'art. First in *OC* (1960, XVII).

Les Aventures de Sophie. Paris: Gallimard, 1937 (XIX).

La Cantate à trois voix, in *Cette Heure qui est entre le printemps et l'été.* Paris: Gallimard, 1913 (I).

Le Cantique des cantiques publ. originally as *Paul Claudel interroge LE CANTIQUE DES CANTIQUES.* Paris-Fribourg: Egloff, 1948 (XXII).

Cent Phrases pour éventails. Tokyo: Koshiba, 1927 (IV).

Cinq Grandes Odes, with *Processionnal pour saluer le siècle nouveau.* Paris: L'Occident, 1910 (I).

Connaissance de l'Est. Paris: Mercure de France, 1900 (III).

Contacts et circonstances. Paris: Gallimard, 1947 (XVI).

Conversations dans le Loir-et-Cher. Paris: Gallimard, 1935 (XVI).

Corona benignitatis anni Dei. Paris: Gallimard, 1915 (I).

Correspondence:

Correspondance avec Lugné-Poe [1910-1928], in *Cahier Paul Claudel V.*

Correspondance Paul Claudel-Darius Milhaud [1912-1953], in *Cahier Paul Claudel III.*

Lettres de P. Claudel sur la bible au R.P.R. Paroissien [17 août 1949-11 octobre 1954]. Paris: Debresse, 1955.

Correspondance Paul Claudel-André Gide [1899-1926]. Paris: Gallimard, 1949.

Correspondance Paul Claudel-Francis Jammes-Gabriel Frizeau [1897-1938]. Paris: Gallimard, 1952.

Correspondance Jacques Rivière-Paul Claudel [1907-1914]. Paris: Plon, 1926.

A. du Sarment. *Lettres inédites de mon parrain Paul Claudel* [1925-1955]. Paris. J. Gabalda, 1959.

Correspondance André Suarès-Paul Claudel [1904-1938]. Paris: Gallimard, 1951.

Correspondances avec Copeau, Dullin, Jouvet, in *Cahier Paul Claudel VI.*

Discours et remerciements. Paris: Gallimard, 1947 (XVIII).

Dodoitzu. Paris: Gallimard, 1945 (IV).

Du sens figuré de l'Ecriture, a preface to l'abbé Tardif de Moidrey's *Introduction au LIVRE DE RUTH.* Paris: Desclée de Brouwer, 1938 (XXI).

L'Echange. 1893-1894 version in collection *L'Arbre*—Paris: Mercure de France, 1901 (VIII). 1950-1951 version in *L'ECHANGE, première et seconde versions*—Paris: Mercure de France, 1954 (VIII).

Ecrits divers. First in *OC* (1952, IV).

Emmaüs. Paris: Gallimard, 1949 (XXIII).

L'Endormie. Paris: Edouard Champion et Daniel Jacomet, 1925 (VI).

L'Epée et le miroir. Paris: Gallimard, 1939 (XX).

L'Evangile d'Isaïe. Paris: Gallimard, 1951 (XXIV).

Feuilles de saints. Paris: Gallimard, 1925 (II).

Figures et paraboles. Paris: Gallimard, 1936 (V).

L'Histoire de Tobie et de Sara. Paris: Gallimard, 1942 (XIV).

L'Homme et son désir. Privately publ. in Brazil, 1917 (XIII).

Introduction à l'APOCALYPSE. Paris: Egloff, 1946 (XXI).

J'aime la Bible. Paris: Arthème Fayard, 1955 (XXI).

Jeanne d'Arc au bûcher. Paris: Gallimard, 1939 (XIV).

Le Jet de pierre, in *Théâtre II* (Pléiade). Paris: Gallimard, 1949 (XIV).

La Jeune Fille Violaine. 1892-1893 version—Paris: Excelsior, 1924 (VII). 1898-1900 version in collection *L'Arbre*—Paris: Mercure de France, 1901 (VII).

Journal, 2 vols. Paris: Gallimard, 1968-9. La Bibliothèque de la Pléiade.

Le Livre de Christophe Colomb. Vienna: Edition Universelle, 1929 (XIV).

Le Livre de Job. Paris: Plon, 1946 (XXI).

La Lune à la recherche d'elle-même, in *Théâtre II* (Pléiade). Paris: Gallimard, 1949 (XIV).

Mémoires improvisés. Paris: Gallimard, 1954. While the 1954 version is used for references the 1969 version (no. 190 in Gallimard's "Collection Idées") is more complete and more accurate; in this sense it too is a "first publication."

La Messe là-bas. Paris: Gallimard, 1919 (II).

Une Mort prématurée (or *Fragment d'un drame*), in Benoist-Mechin's *Bibliographie des oeuvres de Paul Claudel*. Paris: Auguste Blaizot, 1931 (VI).

La Nuit de Noël 1914, publ. with *Poèmes de guerre*. Paris: Gallimard, 1922 (XIII).

L'OEil écoute. Paris: Gallimard, 1946 (XVII).

OEuvres complètes, XXVI volumes to date. Paris: Gallimard, 1950-1967.

L'Oiseau noir dans le soleil levant. Paris: Gallimard, 1929 (III).

Oresteia translation. *Agamemnon*—Foochow: Chez la veuve Rozario, 1896 (VIII). *Les Choéphores*—Paris: Gallimard, 1920 (VIII). *Les Euménides*—Paris: Gallimard, 1920 (VIII).

L'Otage. Paris: Gallimard, 1911 (X).

L'Ours et a lune. Paris: Gallimard, 1919 (XIII).

Le Pain dur. Paris: Gallimard, 1918 (X).

Partage de midi. 1905 version—Paris: L'Occident, 1906 (XI). 1948 version ("version pour la scène")—first in *OC* (1957, XI). 1949 version ("nouvelle version pour la scène")—Paris: Gallimard, 1949 (XI).

Paul Claudel interroge l'APOCALYPSE. Paris: Gallimard, 1952 (XXV).

Le Père humilié. Paris: Gallimard, 1920 (X).

Petits Poèmes d'après le chinois. First in *OC* (1952, IV).

Poèmes de guerre. This *OC* collection (1952, II) includes the following collections, previously publ.: *Trois poèmes de guerre* (Paris: Gallimard, 1915); *Poèmes de guerre* (Paris: Gallimard, 1922); *Ainsi donc encore une fois* (Paris: Gallimard, 1940); *Poèmes et paroles durant la guerre de trente ans* (Paris: Gallimard, 1945).

Un Poète regarde la Croix. Paris: Gallimard, 1938 (XIX).

Positions et propositions. *I*—Paris: Gallimard, 1928 (XV). *II*—Paris: Gallimard, 1934 (XV).

Premiers Vers. First in *OC* (1950, I).

Présence et prophétie. Fribourg: Egloff, 1942 (XX).

Protée, publ. with *La Cantate à trois voix* under title of *Deux Poèmes d'été*. Paris: Gallimard, 1914 (XIII).

Psaumes. Paris: Desclée de Brouwer, 1966.

Le Ravissement de Scapin, in *Théâtre II* (Pléiade). Paris: Gallimard, 1949 (XIV).

Le Repos du septième jour, in collection *L'Arbre*. Paris: Mercure de France, 1901 (VIII).

La Rose et le rosaire. Paris: Egloff, 1947 (XXI).

La Sagesse ou la parabole du festin. Paris: Ronald Davis, 1926 (XIII).

Seigneur, apprenez-nous à prier. Paris: Gallimard, 1942 (XXIII).

Le Soulier de satin. 1919-1924 version—Paris: Gallimard, 1928-1929 (XII). 1942-1943 version ("version pour la scène")—Paris: Gallimard, 1944 (XII).

Sous le rempart d'Athènes. Paris: Gallimard, 1927 (XIII).

Sous le signe du dragon. Paris: La Table Ronde, 1948 (IV).

Tête d'or. 1889 version—Paris: L'Art Indépendant, 1890 (VI). 1894 version in collection *L'Arbre*—Paris: Mercure de France, 1901 (VI).

Trois Figures saintes pour le temps actuel. Paris: Le Livre Contemporain, Amyot-Dumont, 1953 (XXIV).

Vers d'exil, in *Théâtre V.* Paris: Mercure de France, 1912 (I).

La Ville. 1890 version—Paris: L'Art Indépendant, 1903 (VII). 1897 version in collection *L'Arbre*—Paris: Mercure de France, 1901 (VII).

Visages radieux. Paris: Egloff, 1947 (II).

Part II: *CLAUDEL IN ENGLISH TRANSLATION*

The book of Christopher Columbus. Transl. by the author with the help of Agnes Meyer and Darius Milhaud. Publ. jointly by Yale University Press (New Haven) and Oxford University Press (London) in 1930.

Break of noon. Transl. by Wallace Fowlie. Chicago: Regnery, 1960 (Gateway pocketbook #6058). *See Two dramas.*

The city (both versions). Transl. by John Strong Newberry. New Haven: Yale University Press, 1920.

Coronal (*Corona benignitatis anni Dei*). Transl. by Sister Mary David. New York: Pantheon, 1943.

Crusts (*Le Pain dur*). Transl. by John Heard. Boston: Branden. See *Three plays.*

The East I know. Transl. by Teresa Frances and William Rose Benét. New Haven: Yale University Press, 1914.

The essence of the Bible (*J'aime la Bible*). Transl. by Wade Baskin. New York: Philosophical Library, 1957.

The eye listens. Transl. by Elsie Pell. New York: Philosophical Library, 1950.

Five great odes. Transl. by E. Lucie-Smith. London: Rapp and Carroll, 1967.

The hostage. Transl. by Pierre Chavannes. New Haven: Yale University Press, 1917.

The hostage. Transl. by John Heard. Boston: Branden. See *Three plays.*

The humiliation of the Father. Transl. by John Heard. Boston: Branden. See *Three plays.*

I believe in God (Je crois en Dieu). Transl. by Helen Weaver. New York: Holt, Rinehart and Winston, 1963. Then, London: Harvill, 1965.

Letters from Paul Claudel, my godfather. Transl. by William Howard. Westminster, Md.: Newman, 1964.

Letters to a doubter (Correspondance Jacques Rivière-Paul Claudel). Transl. by Henry Longan Stuart. New York: A. & C. Boni, 1927.

Lord, teach us how to pray. Transl. by Ruth Bethell. New York: Longmans, Green, 1948

Paul Claudel-André Gide: The correspondence. Transl. by John Russell. New York: Pantheon, 1952 (subsequently, Beacon Paperbacks BP175).

A poet before the Cross. Transl. by Wallace Fowlie. Chicago: Regnery, 1958.

Poetic art. Transl. by Renée Spodheim. New York: Philosophical Library, 1948.

The satin slipper. Transl. by the Rev. Fr. John O'Connor. London: Sheed and Ward, 1931. New York: Sheed and Ward, 1945.

Tête d'or (second version). Transl. by John Strong Newberry. New Haven: Yale University Press, 1916.

The tidings brought to Mary. Transl. by Louise Morgan Sill. New Haven: Yale University Press, 1916.

The tidings brought to Mary. Transl. by Wallace Fowlie. Chicago: Regnery, 1960 (Gateway pocketbook #6062). See *Two dramas*.

Three plays; The hostage, Crusts, The humiliation of the Father. Transl. by John Heard. Boston: John W. Luce, 1945. See individual titles for subsequent Branden releases.

Three poems of the war (Trois Poèmes de guerre, now part of *Poèmes de guerre)*. Transl. by Edward J. O'Brien. New Haven: Yale University Press, 1919.

Two dramas; Break of noon, The tidings brought to Mary. Transl. by Wallace Fowlie. Chicago: Regnery, 1960. See individual titles for simultaneous release as Gateway pocketbooks.

Ways and crossways (Positions et propositions I). Transl. by the Rev. Fr. John O'Connor. New York: Sheed and Ward, 1933.

Part III: Secondary Sources

ANTOINE, GERALD. *Les CINQ GRANDES ODES de Claudel ou la poésie de la répétition*. Paris: Lettres Modernes, 1959. Important as a first step toward the thorough thematic study that must come.

BEAUMONT, ERNEST. *L'Ode claudélienne—deux exégètes*. Paris: Lettres Modernes, 1958. Valuable appraisal of the studies by Maurocordato and van Hoorn, *q.v.*

————. *The theme of Beatrice in the plays of Paul Claudel.* London: Rockliff, 1954. Translated into French by Huguette Foster: *Le Sens de l'amour dans le théâtre de Claudel.* Paris: Lettres Modernes, 1958. A thorough presentation of an important aspect.

BERCHAN, RICHARD. *The inner stage: an essay on the conflict of vocations in the early works of Paul Claudel.* East Lansing: Michigan State University Press, 1966. Historically interesting for being the first book-length study on conflicts or tensions.

BOLY, JOSEPH, O.S.C. *L'ANNONCE FAITE A MARIE—étude et analyse.* Paris: Les Editions de l'Ecole, 1957. Impressive spadework on the sources and development of the Violaine plays.

BRUNEL, PIERRE. *LE SOULIER DE SATIN devant la critique—dilemme et controverses.* Paris: Lettres Modernes, 1964. Fascinating presentation of the critical reception of one play.

BUCHER, BERNADETTE. "L'Arrière-plan amérindien de *L'Echange.*" *La Table Ronde,* no. 194 (March 1964), 112-33. Subsequent form of same article: "Paul Claudel et le monde amérindien," in *Claudel et l'Amérique (Cahier Canadien Claudel 2),* pp. 85-121. Much surprising and valuable information on the Indian *motif* of the play.

BULLETINS DE LA SOCIETE PAUL CLAUDEL. Almost forty have appeared between 1958 and 1970. Issued by the Société (13, rue du Pont-Louis-Philippe, Paris 4ᵉ), the bulletins are of extreme interest and value to Claudelians.

CAHIERS CANADIENS CLAUDEL 1-6. Ottawa: University of Ottawa, 1963-1969. The subtitles to date indicate the vital use and interest of this series: *1—L'ENDORMIE de Paul Claudel ou la naissance du génie; 2—Claudel et l'Amérique I; 3—Claudel et l'Allemagne; 4—Géographie poétique de Claudel; 5—Formes et figures; 6—Claudel et l'Amérique II.* Margaret Andersen is author of volume 3, Eugène Roberto is author of volume I and also editor of series.

CAHIERS PAUL CLAUDEL I-VIII. Paris: Gallimard, 1959-1968. The subtitles to date indicate their great value and interest: *I—TETE D'OR et les débuts littéraires; II—Le Rire de Paul Claudel;—III—Correspondance Paul Claudel-Darius Milhaud; IV—Claudel diplomate; V—Claudel homme de théâtre* and *Correspondance avec Lugné-Poe; VI—Claudel homme de théâtre* and *Correspondances avec Copeau, Dullin, Jouvet; VII—La Figure d'Israël; VIII—Claudel et l'univers chinois.* Vol. VIII, a monograph by Gilbert Gadoffre, is especially valuable.

CHAIGNE, LOUIS. *Vie de Paul Claudel et genèse de son oeuvre.* Paris: Mame, 1962. Avoid error-ridden 1961 edition. Despite author's "I-knew-him-when" tone, one cannot overlook this well-illustrated and sensitive life. However, pay no attention to second half of title.

CHIARI, JOSEPH. *The poetic drama of Paul Claudel.* London: Harvill, 1954. That the author is not a thorough admirer is refreshing, though some of his reservations exasperate.

CLAUDEL NEWSLETTER 1-4. Kingston, Rhode Island: University of Rhode Island, 1968-1969. Stresses Claudel's connections with America.

CUNNEEN, JOSEPH E. "The present state of Claudel criticism." *Thought,* volume XXVII, no. 107 (winter 1952-1953), pp. 500-20. Alas, no like study of comparable worth has appeared since.

FARABET, RENE. *Le Jeu de l'acteur dans le théâtre de Claudel.* Paris: Lettres Modernes, 1960. Vital for the back pages and their "Représentations des oeuvres théâtrales de Claudel," which list what, when, who, of all professional performances between 1912 and 1959.

FOWLIE, WALLACE. *Claudel.* London: Bowes and Bowes, 1957. Of great worth for the explanation of certain Catholic aspects.

GUILLEMIN, HENRI *Claudel et son art d'écrire.* Paris: Gallimard, 1955. A good and objective style study.

GUYARD, MARIUS-FRANCOIS. *Recherches claudéliennes autour des CINQ GRANDES ODES.* Paris: C. Klincksieck, 1963. One of a few good overall presentations.

HUBERT, RENEE RIESE. "Claudel, poète en prose." *The French Review,* volume XXXV, no. 4 (Feb. 1962), 369-76. Very good discussion of Claudel's prose-poetry.

LASERRE, PIERRE. *Les Chapelles littéraires.* Paris: Garnier, 1920. The study opposes "cultist" literature in general. It is intriguing to hear the other side so vehemently stated. Pp. 1-70 and part of introduction directly concern Claudel.

LESORT, PAUL-ANDRE. *Paul Claudel par lui-même.* Paris: Seuil, 1963 ("Ecrivains de Toujours #63"). The best short life. An amazing treasury of bibliographical data.

MADAULE, JAQUES. *Le Drame de Paul Claudel,* "édition entièrement mise à jour." Paris: Desclée de Brouwer, 1964. This study is and always will be a sort of bible on its subject.

————. *Le Génie de Paul Claudel.* Paris: Desclée de Brouwer, 1933. Full of insights on Claudel's production up to the early 1930's.

MATHESON, WILLIAM. *Claudel and Aeschylus.* Ann Arbor: The University of Michigan Press, 1965. An able indepth study of the connections, sure, probable, possible. The richest presentation that there is on the exact nature of Claudel's studies at Louis-le-Grand.

MAUROCORDATO, ALEXANDRE. *L'Ode de Paul Claudel—essai de phénoménologie littéraire.* Geneva-Lille: Droz-Giard, 1955. Especially valuable on structure of the *verset.*

O'DONNELL, DONAT. *Maria Cross.* New York: Oxford University Press, 1952. Pp. 167-200 deal exclusively with Claudel, but they should not be read apart from the rest of the book, for all of its sections concern the interesting theses on Catholic symbolism that are drawn toward the end.

PAUL CLAUDEL 1-5. Paris: Lettres Modernes, 1964-1968. Excellent series edited by the most Claudelian Jacques Petit. Each issue organized round a theme. Titles to date: *1—Quelques Influences formatrices; 2—"Le Regard en arrière"* (on play versions); *3— Thèmes et images; 4—Claudel et l'histoire; 5—Schémas dramatiques.*

PEYRE, HENRI. "Le Classicisme de Paul Claudel." *La Nouvelle Revue Française,* volume XXXIX, no. 228 (Sept. 1932), 432-41. An early and ever-fresh presentation of the subject.

SPITZER, LEO. "Interpretation of an ode by Paul Claudel," in his *Linguistics and literary history.* Princeton: Princeton University Press, 1948. Pp. 193-236. There are few studies of Claudel's poetry of this caliber. The passage studied is from "La Muse qui est la Grâce."

————. "A linguistic and literary interpretation of Claudel's 'Ballade.'" *The French Review,* vol. XVI, no. 2 (December 1942), 134-43. Same comment as preceding one on this study of the 1917 *Feuilles de saints* poem.

VACHON, ANDRE. *Le Temps et l'espace dans l'oeuvre de Paul Claudel.* Paris: Seuil, 1965. Good study of Claudel as both a death (Easter) and birth (Christmas) writer.

VAN HOORN, H.J.W., O.F.M. *Poésie et mystique—Paul Claudel, poète chrétien.* Geneva-Paris: Droz-Minard, 1957. Fine presentation of Catholic aspects of poetry.

Index

172

PAUL CLAUDEL